CITYPACK
Shanghai

By Christopher Knowles

Fodor's

Fodor's Travel Publications, Inc.
New York • Toronto • London • Sydney • Auckland

WWW.FODORS.COM

Contents

About this book...4

About this book

KEY TO SYMBOLS

🞣 map reference on the fold-out map accompanying this book (see below)

✉ address

☎ telephone number

🕐 opening times

🍴 restaurant or café on premises or nearby

Ⓜ nearest subway station

🚉 nearest train station

🚌 nearest bus route

⛴ nearest riverboat or ferry stop

♿ facilities for visitors with disabilities

✋ admission charge

↔ other nearby places of interest

❓ tours, lectures, or special events

▶ cross-reference (see below)

ℹ tourist information

ORGANIZATION

Citypack Shanghai's six sections cover the six most important aspects of your visit to Shanghai.

- Shanghai life—the city and its people
- Itineraries, walks, evening strolls and excursions—how to organize your time
- The top 25 sights to visit, plotted west–east
- Features about different aspects of the city that make it special
- Detailed listings of restaurants, hotels, shops and nightlife
- Practical information

In addition, text boxes provide fascinating extra facts and snippets, highlights of places to visit and invaluable practical advice.

CROSS-REFERENCES

To help you make the most of your visit, cross-references, indicated by ▶ , show you where to find additional information about a place or subject.

MAPS

- **The fold-out map** in the wallet at the back of the book is a comprehensive street plan of Shanghai. All the map references given in the book refer to this map. For example, the Jade Buddha Temple has the following information: 🞣 G3 – indicating the grid square of the map in which the Jade Buddha Temple will be found.

- **The city-center maps** found on the inside front and back covers of the book itself are for quick reference. They show the Top 25 Sights, described on pages 26–50, which are clearly plotted by number (**❶** – **㉕**, not page number) from west to east.

PRICES

Where appropriate, an indication of the cost of an establishment is given by **$** signs: **$$$** denotes higher prices, **$$** denotes average prices, while **$** denotes lower charges.

SHANGHAI
life

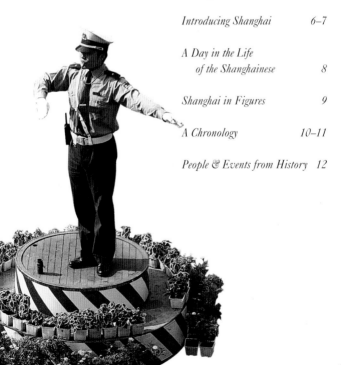

INTRODUCING SHANGHAI

A word of advice

Shanghai is one of the fastest-changing cities in the world. Visitors should be aware that hotels, restaurants, clubs and bars can close, move or change name more rapidly than in most cities. In addition, few people speak English, except in tourist hotels. If you wish to visit any establishment listed in this guide, you are advised to ask a member ot staff at your hotel to telephone and check that it is still open and at the same address.

Shanghailanders

The pre-war generations of European and American expatriates called themselves "Shanghailanders." It is a measure of how much things have changed in recent years that there is again a thriving expatriate community who occasionally refer to themselves by this name.

In the early 1980s, a visitor arriving in Shanghai from Hong Kong would have been aware of the enormous contrast between the two great cities. Hong Kong had by then shed almost every physical vestige of its colonial past while Shanghai had barely altered since the "Shanghailanders" (▶ panel below) had departed in the mid-1940s, leaving behind a vast museum of early 20th-century Western architecture. Villas had been broken up into tiny apartments to house the huge population, the statues of civic dignitaries torn down, and the glitter and neon extinguished. Shanghai was pervaded by the gloom of neglect, but a former resident returning 50 years on would have found the shell of the city perfectly intact. The soul had fled but the corpse was preserved.

Twenty years ago, the Park Hotel, half way along the Nanking Road, was the tallest building in China—hard to believe now, dwarfed as it is by ranks of modern skyscrapers. A visitor then would be likely to stay in the Peace Hotel, on the Bund, the city's waterfront, in rooms with cavernous trunk cupboards and fixtures and plumbing—rather creaky by then—from the hotel's heyday. There was the Hengshan, with its silver-plated breakfast service, and Shanghai Mansions, overlooking Suzhou Creek (Wusong River) and what was then the Soviet Consulate. The first Friendship Store (▶ 45) was in the grounds of the old British Consulate, which was where the modern story of Shanghai began.

Now Shanghai is surrounded by an extraordinary network of expressways to cope with the traffic, and the neon has been switched back on with a vengeance. The Park and Peace hotels still stand but have been exuberantly modernized while spanking new, luxury hotels have mushroomed across the city. Pudong, for long an empty wasteland opposite the Bund, has been transmogrified. The rich in Shanghai are now local people, constantly on shopping sprees in stores overflowing with imported goods. The city has sprung back into life.

Shanghai clings to its status as the fashionable center of China. Consciously or unconsciously, symbols of its pre-war notoriety constantly reappear—several skyscrapers have adopted the distinctive pyramidical roof of the Peace Hotel, for example. More importantly for the visitor, although the old model is being slowly dismantled to make way for the new one, the best of the old city, the "paradise for adventurers," is still there. The municipal authorities have recognized that the infamy of old Shanghai is more than part of the lure for visitors. The happy consequence is that Shanghai's history can still be read on the streets.

The Nanking Road—the Fifth Avenue or Oxford Street of China

A DAY IN THE LIFE OF THE SHANGHAINESE

Shanghai has changed a great deal since it opened to the West, but daily life for most people continues largely as it was before.

The day starts early, especially in the summer, when cramped living conditions combine with the oppressive heat to drive people to leave home early. Buses and trolleybuses are soon crowded and the parks and riverside pavements become exercise areas for people practicing tai chi or, increasingly, aerobics.

Working families leave their child in the care of a grandparent, or, if they can afford it, at a boarding nursery from Monday to Friday.

Breakfast might be eaten at home or from a stand on the way to work. It might be rice soup in winter, or noodles, or rice and pickles, or a sort of fried breadstick. It will certainly include tea, which is drunk at various times throughout the day. People often carry a jar in which the same tea leaves, compacted to the bottom, are constantly revived with boiling water.

Worship at temples and churches is once again widely practiced after several decades during which it was prohibited by the authorities. Local temples have reopened and are now crowded throughout the day with incense-waving worshippers.

Business has become the most important feature of modern Shanghai. Go into any restaurant, especially in the new hotels, and you will observe a meeting in progress. Cellular telephones will be in constant use and various minions in attendance. As the offices close for the day, the buses and restaurants fill once again.

The streets, too, will fill with late night shoppers, and on the Nanking and Huaihai roads, hustlers appear at dusk to tempt the unwary with salacious suggestions, in the old Shanghai style.

Rural Shanghai

Although Shanghai is densely populated, the world of paddy fields and mulberry bushes is only a short drive away. Chinese farmers were among the first to prosper once the State abolished the commune system requiring produce to be pooled and sold by the leaders of the commune. Real wealth nowadays is acquired in the city while life in the country is still hard—but farmers can at least reap the rewards of their own labor.

China's entrepreneurs are never without their cellular phones

SHANGHAI IN FIGURES

THE PLACE

- Shanghai lies 31.14° north of the equator, covers an area of 2,448 square miles and is situated on the Huangpu River, only 15 miles upstream of the mighty Yangtse.
- By 1999, more than half of the world's cranes had been drafted into Shanghai during its massive building program.

THE PEOPLE

- Shanghai's population is about 13 million. The 300, 000 annual abortions and the "One Child Family Policy" have stabilized population growth.
- There are about 8 million people employed in Shanghai. Of these, some 62 percent work for state-run enterprises and about 5.5 percent in private business—the suburban rural areas employ the remaining workers.
- Life expectancy has reached that of so-called developed countries, standing at 74.07 years for men, and 78.21 for women.

THE PORT

- Shanghai is the largest port in China, with wharves of a total length of 21,420 yards, accommodating 229 berths, 69 of which can handle ships of 10,000 tons or more.
- In 1984, the port of Shanghai handled more than 100 million tons of cargo, which ranked it among the largest in the world. In 1996, it handled 164 million tons.

Still magnificent—Shanghai's waterfront, the Bund

A Chronology

1300s Shanghai is a fairly important trading center, with a Customs House and it becomes a county seat, under the jurisdiction of Jiangsu Province.

1553 The people of Shanghai build a city wall as, during the Ming dynasty (1368–1644), a flourishing cotton industry develops and Shanghai becomes a target for Japanese pirates.

1842 The Opium Wars reach Shanghai which is sacked by the British. The Treaty of Nanking, signed in August the same year, permits them to undertake unlimited trade (Concessions), in Shanghai and four other coastal cities.

1863 The British and American concessions merge to form the International Settlement, while the French Concession remains autonomous. The foreign community enjoys "extraterritoriality," which places it outside Chinese law.

1890s The International Settlement is thought of as a "Model" Concession. The Shanghai Municipal Council (local government operated by foreigners, which even has the power to bar entry to Chinese troops), operates patrols of Sikh mounted police, organizes thrice daily garbage collections, provides electric and gas, street lighting, and drinking water from the waterworks 3 miles away.

1911 The Qing dynasty falls and China becomes a republic. In 1912, to create more space for the mercantile "paradise" that Shanghai is becoming, the city walls are demolished.

1917 Refugees from the Russian Revolution bring a new style to Shanghai entertainment—with outrageous cabarets competing with the old, sedate ballrooms. The Shanghai of legend, the "whore of the Orient," is born.

1925 Instability. Labor unrest in Japanese-owned cotton mills leads to strikes, dismissals and violence, and new laws unsympathetic to the Chinese unite industrialists with workers. On

May 30, clashes between students and police result in several deaths. The "May 30 Incident" is to become part of Communist lore.

1927 The foreign community permits the Nationalist leader Chiang Kai Shek to move troops against the Communists through the foreign concessions. On April 12, 1,000 Nationalists attack the Communists in Chapei (Zhabei). Twenty die, and several hundred, including Zhou En Lai who manages to escape, are arrested (145 are later executed).

1930s Japan occupies Shanghai and remains in power until the end of World War II.

1949 Mao becomes leader of China, and Communist troops enter Shanghai. Few foreigners remain, but it is the beginning of the end for the Shanghai of excess and the end of an era in the most important business and trading center in Asia.

1966 The beginning of the Cultural Revolution, a period of brutality and terror. Shanghai, China's most industrialized and politically radical city, is among the first to enter the fray. Violent rebel groups roam the streets, which are renamed with revolutionary fervor.

1972 The Shanghai Communiqué is signed between China and the U.S. in the Jin Jiang Hotel (► 82), signifying the end of China's isolation from the outside world.

1976 Mao dies: The Gang of Four, including Mao's widow, make the city their base in their attempt to seize power.

1990s Shanghai reenters the industrial world, becoming an autonomous municipality running its own affairs. The area of Pudong becomes a Special Economic Zone, where free trade is allowed. Several ministers in the central government, including former mayors Jiang Zemin and Zhu Rongji are from Shanghai.

PEOPLE & EVENTS FROM HISTORY

Sir Robert Hart, a respected figure

The Gang of Four

All four members of the so-called Gang of Four, who tried to seize power following the death of Chairman Mao, had Shanghai connections. Jiang Qing, Mao's last wife, was a Shanghai actress. Chang Chun Qiao had been a journalist and director of propaganda in Shanghai. Yao Wen Yuan had been editor of the newspaper *Shanghai Liberation Army Daily.* Wang Hong Wen had been a Shanghai worker and founder member of the Shanghai Workers Revolutionary Headquarters.

ROBERT HART

Sir Robert Hart was one of the most important figures in the early development of the treaty port of Shanghai. Born in Portadown, Northern Ireland, he was an English/Chinese interpreter before he was invited by the Chinese government to establish a Customs House in Shanghai. Eventually Hart's Customs Service became the financial hub of the government. In 1865, the service was moved to Peking and Hart moved with it. He was one of the few foreigners of the era to be respected by the Chinese, and was given the title of "Guardian of Heir Apparent" when he died in 1911.

THE SOONG FAMILY

The influence of this legendary family reached beyond Shanghai to the national and international stage. There were three sisters: Soong Ai-Ling, married H.H. Kung, a financier descended from Confucius; Soong Mei-Ling married General Chiang Kai Shek who became Taiwan's first leader; and Soong Qing-Ling married Sun Yat Sen, the revolutionary who established the Chinese Republic in 1911. Of the three, it was said that "one loved money, one loved power and one loved China." Their brother, financier T.V. Soong, was Minister of Finance between 1925 and 1933. Later, throughout the 1930s, as Chairman of the Bank of China, he wielded enormous influence over Shanghai business. He was the richest man of his generation.

THE GANGSTERS

Pre-war Shanghai was an iniquitous place, fully deserving of its soubriquet as the "whore of the Orient." Nothing illustrates this better than the roles played by the gangsters, Pockmarked Huang (Huang Jinrong) and Big-eared Du (Du Yuesheng), who ran protection rackets, organized drug smuggling and controlled the city's many prostitutes. Du would warn the targets of his protection rackets of the dangers of Shanghai life by delivering a coffin to their door. Huang enjoyed perfect immunity—he was also Chief Detective for the French Sûreté.

SHANGHAI
how to organize your time

ITINERARIES

Although Shanghai is a huge city, many interesting sites are concentrated in a fairly small central area comprising the original Chinese town and the former French and International Concessions. Four days are ample for seeing the best of the city, and the best means of getting around are by taxi and on foot.

ITINERARY ONE	**THE WATERFRONT**
Morning	Start at the Peace Hotel (► 46) to soak up the flavor of pre-war Shanghai. Walk along the Bund and the waterfront, perhaps paying a visit to the huge Friendship Store (► 45) on Beijing Lu.
Afternoon	Go for a cruise on the Huangpu River (► 50) passing through the port area as far as the confluence with the Yangtse.
Evening	Have a meal in the Peace Hotel (► 46) and then go downstairs to the bar to hear its renowned jazz band.
ITINERARY TWO	**THE OLD TOWN**
Morning	Head for Yuyuan (Yu Garden ► 42) on the edge of the Old Town (► 43) and relax with a traditional pot of Chinese tea in the Huxingting Tea House (► 44), just outside the garden.
Afternoon	Wander the narrow old streets of the Old Town, with their popular dumpling restaurants and antique and jewelry stores.
Evening	Finish your day with a meal in the Lao Fandian (► 64), a well-known restaurant in the Old Town, or one of the many restaurants along nearby Huaihai Lu.
ITINERARY THREE	**SOUTHWEST SHANGHAI**
Morning	In the southwest corner of the city, see a grandiose piece of old Shanghai in the form of the Catholic Cathedral at Xujiahui (► 26). By contrast, not far from here, is the Longhua

Dumplings, the best fast food in the world

Pagoda (➤ 30), part of a Buddhist temple, which has a vegetarian restaurant where you can have lunch.

Afternoon Continue farther south through Shanghai's suburbs to stroll through the Botanical Gardens (➤ 29), and view its colorful displays of bonsai trees and shrubs.

Evening After an early dinner in one of the Nanking Road restaurants (or in the Park Hotel ➤ 84), catch a performance by the widely admired Shanghai Acrobatic Troupe.

ITINERARY FOUR **CENTRAL SHANGHAI**

Morning Visit the magnificent collection of bronzes, porcelain and paintings in Shanghai's new museum (➤ 38) on People's Square. On your way to the Jade Buddha Temple (➤ 32), stop for lunch and shopping in the old Exhibition Center (➤ 33).

Afternoon Head for the Jade Buddha Temple to see local people at worship and to enjoy the tranquil Buddha exquisitely sculpted in jade.

Evening After dinner in one of many restaurants in the center of the city, spend an hour or two in the revitalized Great World entertainment center (➤ 40).

15

WALKS

Tai chi on the Bund

THE BUND & THE NANKING ROAD

Obtain a feeling for old Shanghai by taking a walk along the two best known thoroughfares of Shanghai. The Bund, or the waterfront, was where the story of Shanghai began, while the Nanking Road (Nanjing Lu) is still the most famous shopping street in China (➤ 41).

Start at the Park Hotel roughly where Nanking Road East (Nanjing Donglu) meets Nanking Road West (Nanjing Xilu). At the time of its construction in the 1930s, the Park was the tallest building in Asia. Turn left out of the hotel onto the Nanking Road, with the clock tower of the old racetrack behind you. Walk past a number of buildings which date from the Concession days and innumerable stores and department stores, including the old Wing On, Sincere, and Sun Sun.

THE SIGHTS

- Nanking Road (➤ 41)
- International Settlement (➤ 39)
- Peace Hotel (➤ 46)
- The Bund (➤ 48)
- Friendship Store (➤ 45)
- Huangpu River (➤ 50)

INFORMATION

Distance 2½ miles
Time 1½ hours (not including visits)
Start point Park Hotel
🚇 J5
🚌 Bus 20, 27
End point Dong Feng Hotel
🚇 K5
🚌 Bus 22, 42, 55, 65

After about 45 minutes of continuous walking you will come to the Bund, with the main building of the Peace Hotel on your left, and its older wing (the former Palace Hotel) on the right. The Huangpu River lies beyond the Bund, just in front of you.

Turn left to walk along the Bund, passing a number of pre-war European style buildings including the original headquarters of the former opium traders, Jardine Matheson, and the old British Consulate. The Friendship Store is just along Beijing Lu on the left. At the Waibaidu Bridge, cross to the riverside embankment and return along the Bund for a view of the river and the impressive arc of the Bund.

Pass the Peace Hotel again and the intersection of the Nanking Road and continue to the end of the Bund opposite the Dong Feng Hotel, the old Shanghai Club.

THE OLD TOWN

Long before the Europeans and Americans arrived in the mid-19th century to create one of the greatest cities in the world, in terms of its size and trading power, Shanghai was a busy, walled town. Many old buildings remain and you will see some of them on this walk.

Start from Dongmen Lu, the site of the old east gate to the Chinese town, close to the waterfront. Walk westwards, and pass Waixiangua Jie (Salty Melon Street), with its local food market. Continue to Zhonghua Lu—cross the street to enter Fangbang Zhonglu, with an interesting traditional Chinese medicine pharmacy on the corner. Continue past a variety of stores until an old Chinese arch appears to the right, the entrance to the Temple of the City God which once formed what is left of the old town (the temple no longer exists). This is the area which most retains something of a traditional atmosphere conveyed through its architecture and stores. Go through the arch and find your way among the stores and restaurants until you come to the lake and the Huxingting Tea House, or Mid-Lake Pavilion, near the entrance to the Yu Garden. Bear right around the lake and then turn left to wander among the narrow streets before bearing right to leave this area and emerge onto Fuyou Lu. Turn left here and left again onto Jiujiaochang Lu. A street on the right (Chenxiangge Lu) takes you to a small neighborhood temple. Return to Jiujiaochang and continue past stalls and stores to Fangbang Zhonglu. Turn right until you reach the new permanent antiques market on the right. This is at the corner of Henan Lu, where you can find a bus or a taxi, or from where you can walk to Huaihai Lu in the French Concession.

THE SIGHTS

- Old Town (➤ 43)
- Huxingting Tea House/Mid-Lake Pavilion (➤ 44)
- Yu Garden (➤ 42)
- Antiques Market (➤ 56)

INFORMATION

Distance 1½ miles
Time 1 hour excluding stops
Start point Dongmen Lu
✚ L6
🚌 11
End point Fangbang Zhonglu

Traditional pharmacy in the Old Town, a glimpse of old China

EVENING STROLLS

The illuminated Bund—
nightlife returns to
Shanghai

THE BUND/ZHAPU LU

Start at the Peace Hotel (➤ 46) at the intersection of the Bund and the Nanking Road. The bar in the hotel is home to a popular jazz band, so you may prefer to postpone a visit here until after your stroll, when you can sit and enjoy the music. Cross the Bund to the river side (using an underpass) for views of the illuminations, and the passersby along the promenade, and of the river. Turn left and continue to the end, wandering through Huangpu Park if it is still open. Turn back and cross the street to Beijing Lu. Arrive at the Friendship Store (➤ 45) for late night shopping. Then continue to Huqiu Lu (second right) and turn right. Cross the river and wander along Zhapu Lu with its array of neon-lit, good value restaurants.

PEOPLE'S SQUARE, YUNNAN LU, GREAT WORLD

Start from the Park Hotel on the Nanking Road. Cross the street and turn right and then left, by the racecourse clock, into Huangpi Beilu. Continue on Huangpi Beilu (passing, first right, the Flower and Bird Market, ➤ 36) until you come to the broad expanse of People's Square (Renmin Square) once a racetrack, and used for marches and parades during the Cultural Revolution. Turn left here and walk across it, with the new Shanghai Museum (➤ 38) at the far end. Continue in this direction to busy Xizang Zhonglu. Cross and turn right to cross Yan'an Donglu and reach the Great World Center (➤ 40) on the left. Turn left after this into Ninghai Donglu and then left or right into Yunnan Nanlu, where you'll find a large number of restaurants of all types—the ideal spot to end your stroll.

ORGANIZED SIGHTSEEING

TOUR COMPANIES

Just about all organized tourism in Shanghai is still in the hands of CITS (China International Travel Service), the state-owned tour operator and travel agent. CITS has never enjoyed the best reputation, although it has improved a great deal since the late 1970s. In fact, many of the complaints laid at the feet of CITS in those days—hotel quality, an inefficient national airline—were outside their control.

CITS does, however, organize tours of Shanghai which may be useful if you don't have much time. Their head office is located on the 8th floor No. 1277 Beijing Lu (☎ 6321 7200) and there is a branch on Nanjing Donglu, next to the Peace Hotel. CITS can also organize a private guide for the day, although if you hang around long enough on any major thoroughfare, entrepreneurs will probably offer their services. However, if you want to visit certain places—factories or the Children's Palace, for example—CITS is probably unavoidable.

Arrival and departure in Shanghai can be arranged through tour operators at home, and nowadays hotels can be booked directly. Also, major hotels also often organize tours—ask at reception. Other companies (still under the control of CITS) include the Huating Overseas Tourist Corporation, Shanghai Hotel, Wulumuqi Beilu (☎ 6249 1234 or 6248 0088 ext.4407) and the China Comfort Travel Service, Tower 1, Chang'an Building, 1001 Chang'an Lu (☎ 6317 4249).

Bus tour

A possible option for general sightseeing would be to join the Jin Jiang Tour Bus which runs all day making several stops for a very reasonable fee. It starts from the Jin Jiang Hotel at 59 Maoming Nanlu (☎ 6270 1667).

China's tour company logos are widely advertised

EXCURSIONS

INFORMATION

Suzhou

Distance 50 miles west of Shanghai

Time 1¼ hours

🚆 Regular trains from Shanghai's main station, or the West Station.

🚉 CITS can arrange tickets to Suzhou and a guide on arrival. Tickets should be bought in advance. CITS ✉ 8th floor No. 1277 Beijing Lu ☎ 6321 7200. Or try the ticket office in the Longmen Hotel ✉ 77 Hengfeng Lu ☎ No telephone reservations available

INFORMATION

Nanjing

Distance 186 miles northwest of Shanghai

✈ There are daily flights to Nanjing. Flying time is about 40 minutes

🚆 Trains with air-conditioned carriages depart daily. Journey time is 4 hours approx. Tickets should be bought well in advance

🚉 CITS (✉ 8th floor No. 1277 Beijing Lu ☎ 6321 7200) can arrange train or air tickets

SUZHOU

Inland of Shanghai is Suzhou, one of the most beautiful towns in China. This is the China of canals, arched bridges, whitewashed houses and ornamental gardens. Suzhou's prosperity grew with the construction of the Grand Canal during the Sui Dynasty (581–618). By the 12th century, it had reached the dimensions of what is now its historic center and became a noted silk producer. Wealthy merchants built themselves fine villas and gardens, several of which have survived. Highlights here include the North Temple, the Humble Administrator's Garden, the Garden of the Master of the Nets, the Lingering Garden, and the Silk Embroidery Research Institute.

NANJING

Further inland still from Suzhou is Nanjing (Nanking), situated on the Yangtse River. Although a large city with about 4.5 million inhabitants, it has managed to retain something of its old character. It was the first Ming Dynasty capital and, in the 1920s, it became the capital of Nationalist China until the Japanese invasion and the massacre in 1937 known as the Rape of Nanking. Much of the Ming city wall still stands including the impressive Heping and Zhonghua gates. The Nanking River Bridge over the Yangtse is a remarkable piece of engineering, while perhaps the most famous monument in the city is the mausoleum of Sun Yat Sen. There is also an excellent museum, as well as the tomb of the first Ming emperor.

The Sacred Way, protected by symbolic guardians

DIANSHAN HU & THE GRAND VIEW GARDEN

An excursion to Dianshan Lake might include a visit to Qingpu, the county seat, with the Qushui Garden (Crooked Water Garden). The garden was constructed in 1745 and includes a lake, rockeries, pavilions and covered corridors. Close to Qingpu is the town of Zhujiajiao with its canals and old streets. From here to the lake is only 7½ miles. Shangta is the center of the Dianshan Lake Scenic Area. At the lake itself, there are all sorts of leisure activities—a water sports park, swimming pools, a golf course—and the Grand View Garden, a re-creation of the garden that features in the classic Chinese novel, *Dream of Red Mansions*.

SHE SHAN

She Shan is a hill about 25 miles southwest of Shanghai. At its summit, surprisingly, is an imposing, red-brick Catholic church known as "Our Lady of China," where Mass continues to be celebrated in Latin. Its origins go back to the mid-19th century when a wave of xenophobia led to the construction of a small chapel on the remote hillside. An acting bishop of Shanghai, later forced to take refuge here, vowed that in return for protection, he would build a church (the current one dates from 1925). May is a time for pilgrimages when streams of people climb the hill paths which represent the Via Dolorosa.

The busy canal life of Suzhou is a fascinating feature of a visit inland

INFORMATION

Dianshan

Distance 40 miles southwest of Shanghai

🚍 Buses for Qingpu leave regularly from the Western Bus Station

INFORMATION

She Shan

Distance 25 miles

🚍 Take a direct bus from the Xiqu Bus Station, or a bus for Songjiang and descend at the appropriate stop from where you can get a taxi

21

THE YANGTSE GORGES

A short distance from Shanghai is the mouth of China's longest river, the Yangtse, which flows through the heart of the country. At 3,906 miles it is the world's third longest river. The life along its banks is everywhere fascinating, but a highlight of any visit to China must be the spectacular

The Yangtse, where superb scenery and an unchanged way of life meet

cruise through the Yangtse Gorges, which lie in the upper reaches between the great river ports of Chongqing and Wuhan. The Three Gorges (the 5 mile Qutangxia or Bellows Gorge, the 27½ mile Wuxia or Witches Gorge and the 46 mile Xiling Gorge), were formed some 70 million years ago by movements in the earth's crust, which led to the draining of a vast inland sea and the exposure of the perpendicular cliffs.

The construction of the Gezhouba Dam at Yichang has raised the river's level (though not enough to detract too much from the gorges' wild beauty). However, the Chinese government is currently building yet another dam which will, by the year 2010, effectively submerge the gorges for ever.

From Shanghai, it is possible to make the entire voyage to Chongqing by river boat, but the journey as far as Wuhan (where you would probably change boats) is long and scenically uninteresting. The best way of seeing the gorges is to fly to the port of Chongqing, in Sichuan, and take a boat downstream through the gorges to Wuhan.

There are two types of boat plying the route through the gorges. The first is the standard steamer which travels back and forth along the river. These are large and crowded but offer a variety of styles of accommodation, from dormitories to simple twin-bedded cabins. The cost of the trip is about 750 yuan ($100). Food is served to passengers in "soft class" as the Chinese call first class passengers, but it is better to take your own. For example, the Friendship Store sells cookies, fruit, chocolate and dried fruits which might be suitable. The second type of craft, a comparatively recent innovation, is the purpose-built tourist boat. These boats, with well-appointed, air-conditioned cabins with private bathrooms, and good food, make the three-day journey in the summer heat very pleasant, but the cost is at least double that of the ferry.

Crowded boats and ferries ply the Yangtse

Tourist boats make fewer stops than the ferry. However, they do offer the chance to journey up the impressive Lesser Gorges, which flank the Daning River, a tributary of the Yangtse.

Beyond the gorges is the bustling city of Chongqing, worth visiting if only for the food—the spicy cooking of Sichuan is considered by many to be the finest in China—and you can also make a day trip to the wonderful Buddhist grottoes at Dazu. Wuhan, too, has interesting temples and an excellent museum. But it is the life along the river banks, which has barely changed for thousands of years, that makes the trip memorable.

WHAT'S ON

The dates of traditional Chinese festivals vary from year to year according to the lunar calendar, which usually begins in February.

WINTER/SPRING   *Chinese New Year/Spring Festival*—The most important festival in the Chinese calendar, like Christmas and New Year in one, usually falls in February. Red envelopes containing money are given to encourage prosperity. It may be hard to come by hotel rooms at this time and many attractions are closed.

Lantern Festival—Falls on the 15th day of the first lunar month. People buy paper lanterns and walk the streets with them illuminated.

Guanyin's Birthday—Guanyin is the goddess of mercy and on her birthday (the 19th day of the second moon) temples are filled with worshippers.

MARCH   *Marathon Cup*—One of China's major sporting events take place in March; thousands of runners jostle along the Bund.

Longhua Temple Fair—In the third lunar month. Celebration of the founding of the Longhua Temple.

MAY   *International Labor Day*—May 1.

Music Festival—A festival of classical western and traditional music.

JUNE   *Children's Day*—June 1.

AUTUMN   *Mid-Autumn Festival*—This takes place on the 15th day of the 8th moon. It recalls a 14th-century uprising against the Mongols and is now celebrated with Moon cakes, filled with lotus root, dates and sesame.

OCTOBER   *National Day*—October 1. Celebration of the founding of the People's Republic of China.

SHANGHAI's
top 25 sights

The sights are shown on the maps on the inside front cover and inside back cover, numbered **1–25** *from west to east across the city*

Xujiahui Cathedral

In a country of Buddhist, Confucian and Taoist traditions that is now officially atheist, perhaps nothing is more surprising than the twin towers of a red brick neo-Gothic cathedral poking defiantly into the sky in the shadow of gleaming skyscrapers.

Victorian Gothic in the Far East

HIGHLIGHTS

- European Gothic among the skyscrapers
- Idiosyncratic detail

INFORMATION

- ✚ D8
- ✉ 158 Puxi Lu
- ☎ 5637 1328
- 🕐 Daily
- Ⓜ Xujiahui
- 🚌 42, 50
- ♿ None
- 🎫 Free
- ↔ Longhua Temple & Pagoda (➤ 30)
- ❓ Daily services

The Jesuits The influence of Jesuit missionaries was experienced in the Shanghai area from as early as the 16th century. An early convert was one Xu Guangqi, a native of Xujiahui, or "Xu Family Village," which at that time was well outside the original town of Shanghai. Xu, an official in the Imperial library, was baptized Paul. He later bequeathed family land to the Jesuits where an observatory and cathedral would eventually be constructed. Following persecution of the converts, the first church here later became a temple to the god of war. After the Treaty of Nanking (1842), the land was given to the French, and in 1848 a Jesuit settlement was firmly established.

The cathedral The current cathedral of St. Ignatius was built in 1906 with two 115-feet-tall spires and capacity for a congregation of 2,500. The interior includes a number of decorative idiosyncrasies that indicate Buddhist influence —melons feature on the nave columns and, along with stylized bats (a Chinese symbol of happiness), in the windows. Outside, gargoyles fringe the roof and a holy grotto has been built in the garden. Severely damaged during the Cultural Revolution, the cathedral is now a busy place of worship, with services at 5:30, 6, 7 and 8AM on weekdays and an extra 6PM service on Sundays. On Saturdays there is a single evening service at 6PM.

SOONG QING-LING'S RESIDENCE

A visit here is an opportunity to see how the wealthy lived in old Shanghai and to reflect on a vital period in China's modern history. Its former owner, Soong Qing-Ling, remained something of a revolutionary icon despite her family background.

HIGHLIGHTS

- Interesting pre-war villa and garden
- Insight into the personality cult

INFORMATION

- ✚ D6
- ✉ 1843 Huaihai Zhonghlu
- 🕐 Daily 9–11 and 1–4:30
- ☎ 6433 5033
- 🚌 911, 42
- ♿ None
- 💰 Inexpensive
- ↔ Xujiahui Cathedral (➤ 26)

Soong Qing-Ling Born in Shanghai in 1893 to a family (➤ 12) whose business was the printing of bibles, Soong Qing-Ling was introduced to the revolutionary Sun Yat Sen (➤ 35) through her father's connections with secret societies dedicated to the fall of the Qing, China's last imperial dynasty. In 1913, on her way home from the United States where she was educated, she stopped off in Japan. Sun was there, rallying support for the restoration of the republic that he had founded in 1911. She became his secretary and they were married in 1915. After Sun's death, she became disenchanted with his successor Chiang Kai Shek and went to Moscow, returning to help with the anti-Japanese war effort. After the revolution, she held a number of political posts in the government and became a useful symbol for China until her death in 1981.

The residence Soong Qing-Ling's residence in Shanghai between 1948 and 1963, in the heart of the old French Concession, dates from the 1920s, when it was built for a Greek boat captain. The house, an attractive villa in European style, with a pretty garden, has been left as it was on the day that she died. As befits the home of a representative of the people, it is furnished fairly simply, although there is an interesting collection of gifts received from eminent visitors to her home, including a carpet from Mao, and a work in bamboo from Kim Il Sung, the late leader of North Korea.

Soong Qing-Ling, who famously "loved China"

3

CARPET & JADE FACTORIES

China is famous for its arts and crafts, especially for the weaving of carpets and the carving of jade. Shanghai is an important center for both, and you can observe skilled practitioners here.

Carpets Both wool and silk are used to produce carpets. The manufacturing process follows three distinct stages. First comes the weaving process—a demanding skill acquired only after a number of years of training. Most workers are girls (usually young, with acute eyesight and nimble fingers). They sit in front of large looms, with the basic pattern of the carpet sketched out behind the warp. Balls of wool in different colors dangle above their heads, and the girls reach for them as required, then tie knots at lightning speed, every so often tamping down the weft with a heavy metal fork. Stage two is the weeding out of imperfections, and stage three the scissor cutting that puts the design into relief, a Chinese specialty.

Jade This is the stone most associated with China and was much coveted by emperors. It is usually thought to be green, but in fact comes in a variety of colors, although certain shades of green and a cloudy white are considered the most valuable. Jade is rarely worked by hand these days—it is an enormously resistant stone. Though a machine is now generally used, the craft still requires skill, patience and a steady hand. The most famously mystifying skill is that of producing a series of jade balls, each of which revolves perfectly within the next.

Jade is much prized by all Chinese

4

SHANGHAI BOTANICAL GARDENS

Like many once-thriving institutions across China, Shanghai Botanical Gardens suffered much during the disaster that was the Cultural Revolution—if only from neglect. Now work is under way to bring it back to its former beauty.

Years of neglect The journey to Shanghai Botanical Gardens, which lie well outside the city center to the southwest, takes you through the sort of dismal suburbs made up of antiquated factories that once characterized every city in China until the early 1980s. Once you reach the gardens, the blooms, and the palm and bamboo groves have to speak for themselves. While the gardens' basic design is perfectly adequate, years of neglect have, to some extent, allowed nature to take over. Bushes have overgrown and weeds have flourished. There are several small diversions that can be made into woodland where you may discover local fishermen trying their luck in lotus-covered ponds. Attempts are being made to appeal to children—there is a lake and windmill, while a small bus tours the gardens in the summer. There is also a restaurant.

Penjing Garden The most enchanting area is the garden within a garden. There is an additional charge to enter the Penjing Garden (*penjing* is the Chinese word for the art of cultivating miniature trees and shrubs, more usually associated with Japanese gardeners and known as bonsai in the West), but it is worth it. Essentially a garden in the traditional Chinese style, made up of pavilions, courtyards and miniature lakes, it also has dozens of marvellous examples of the art of *penjing*. There is an exhibition room and a number of fine examples of ornamental rockeries in this garden.

Landscaping is a vital element in the Gardens

HIGHLIGHTS

- Bonsai or Penjing Garden
- Ponds of lotus

INFORMATION

⊞	Off map in southwest suburbs
⊠	1110 Long Wu Lu
☎	6451 3369
🕐	Daily 8–5
🍴	Simple restaurant (S/SS) on premises
🚌	56
🚫	None
👤	Inexpensive
↔	Longhua Temple & Pagoda (▶ 30)

LONGHUA TEMPLE & PAGODA

HIGHLIGHTS

- Handsome pagoda
- Active temple

INFORMATION

- D10
- 2853 Longhua Lu
- 6457 1440
- Daily 8–4
- Excellent vegetarian restaurant on premises
- 44
- None
- Inexpensive
- Botanical Gardens (➤ 29), Xujiahui Cathedral (➤ 26)

A monk at the Longhua Temple

"The ancient temple stands tall and proud/The pagoda towers into the cloud/Willows encircle the river village/Streams are reddened by the blooming peach."– from a Tang dynasty poem

The pagoda This pagoda's survival is akin to a miracle—something that smacked so obviously of "old China" should have been a prime target for the marauding Red Guards of the Cultural Revolution. The foundations of the pagoda date from AD 977 (the Song dynasty) and although it has doubtless been rebuilt many times since then, it retains the architectural features of the Song period. Seven storeys and 108 feet high, it is octagonal and made of wood and brick, with "flying" eaves of gray tile. It stands on the site of another pagoda thought to have been built during the period known as The Three Kingdoms (AD 238–251).

The temple According to legend, the Longhua Temple was founded during the Three Kingdoms period by Kang Monk Hui, the eldest son of an eminent minister, who was attracted by this marshy area where "the water and the sky were of one color," and the king of Wu (one of the three kingdoms). In reality, it is more likely that its earliest construction was during the Five Dynasties period (AD 923–979), or possibly in the Tang period (AD 618–907). In any event, the current buildings date from the end of the 19th century, during the final (Qing) dynasty. During World War II, the area was used as a POW camp. After years of neglect, the temple has reopened and there are several dozen monks in residence. The temple and surrounding area are noted for their spring peach blossom.

CHILDREN'S PALACE

In a few places in Shanghai it's possible, with a little imagination, to revisit to the era of excess and opulence of pre-war Shanghai. One such place is the Children's Palace in the old Kadoorie Mansion.

The Marble Hall The Kadoorie Mansion, also known as the Marble Hall, was the former home of one of old Shanghai's wealthiest families. The Kadoories were Sephardic Jews, originally from Baghdad. It is said that their architect had taken advantage of the family's absence abroad—and unlimited funds—to make the building far larger than the family wanted. The simple truth is that the Marble Hall, even with its fairly understated design, is typical of the extravagance of pre-war Shanghai. It remains essentially as it was, with the addition of a Red Star and a couple of Soviet-inspired statues, though the interior has become rather shabby. The Kadoorie family continues to thrive in Hong Kong.

Municipal Children's Palace After the revolution, so-called Children's Palaces were introduced around the country in order to encourage children to take up after-school activities—a particular help for working parents. Today these establishments are aimed at gifted children, the best of whom will eventually go on to various academies and conservatoires. A visit here is a charming and fascinating experience; you will see children of all ages learning to sing, play musical instruments, dance, act, and use computers among other activities. In addition, special performances are sometimes put on for foreign visitors, but even the daily routine is of interest. You should ask at your hotel for information about performances.

HIGHLIGHTS

- Beautiful pre-war building
- Talented children in action

INFORMATION

- ✚ F5
- ✉ 64 Yan'an Xilu
- ☎ 6248 1850
- 🕙 Daily, but book through CITS
- 🚌 48, 71
- ♿ None
- 💰 Inexpensive
- ↔ Shanghai Exhibition Center (➤ 33)
- ❓ Occasional concerts

The Palace is an example of colonial architecture

JADE BUDDHA TEMPLE

HIGHLIGHTS

- Active temple
- Beautiful jade carvings

INFORMATION

- G3
- 170 Anyuan Lu
- 6266 3668
- Daily 8–5
- Excellent vegetarian restaurant
- 105, 106
- None
- Inexpensive
- Regular services

The busiest and most famous of Shanghai temples stands among high-rise buildings and small factories. The reason for, and highlight of, a visit is the jewel-covered Buddha in the library, one of two jade Buddhas within the temple.

The temple The Jade Buddha Temple—or Yu Fo Si—was established in 1882 by a monk from the holy mountain of Putuoshan, in southern China, to house the jade Buddha figures. The temple was abandoned after the fall of the Qing dynasty in 1911, then restored between 1918 and 1928. Closed again in 1949, it was saved from destruction during the Cultural Revolution only through the intervention of Prime Minister Zhou En Lai. Although the temple is not of great architectural merit, it is an impressive example of the south Chinese style, especially the roof of the main hall with its steeply raised eaves and decorative figurines. The temple is particularly worth visiting on the first and fifth days of each lunar month, holy days which attract many worshippers.

The newly restored Great Hall of the Jade Buddha Temple

The jade Buddhas After visiting the main prayer halls with their array of gaudy Heavenly Kings and Bodhisattvas, it is time to see the temple's highlights—two jade statues brought from Burma by Abbott Wei Ken. Each is carved from a single piece of creamy white jade. They are housed separately. The first is a 13 foot-long reclining Buddha, the position adopted by Buddha at the moment of death. The more beautiful figure is in the library. Almost 6½ feet high, it weighs 2,200 pounds and is encrusted with semi-precious stones.

SHANGHAI EXHIBITION CENTER

The gargantuan Shanghai Exhibition Center is a legacy of the period during the 1950s when the Soviet Union was closely allied to China. Yet it stands on the site of the home of one of Shanghai's more colorful characters.

Silas Hardoon Shanghai Exhibition Center stands on an intriguing site of which almost nothing original remains but which sums up the sort of place that Shanghai was before 1949. Silas Hardoon was a penniless Jewish immigrant whose family hailed from Baghdad and who joined the Sassoon company as a wharf night-watchman in the late 19th century. He rose to become manager of Sassoon's Shanghai office and in 1920 left to run his own business, speculating in property and public utilities. He became the richest man in Shanghai, married a Eurasian (when mixed marriages were frowned upon), dabbled in Buddhism and adopted a host of children. They were educated at his house, Hardoon Gardens, 26 acres of Chinese fantasy in the middle of Shanghai, now home to the Exhibition Center.

A Soviet legacy Built in 1955 and surmounted by a large star, the Exhibition Center was known as the Palace of Sino-Soviet Friendship until 1960, when the relationship between China and the Soviet Union soured. It is a confection in the grandiose style that was the hallmark of Soviet architecture, reflecting similar buildings in Moscow and in Beijing. There are impressive fountains close to the front gate and very high chandeliers inside, whose location must create a major problem when it comes to changing light-bulbs. Mainly used today for trade exhibitions, the building also houses a gigantic arts and crafts store and, upstairs, a good restaurant.

Shops at the Center specialize in arts and crafts

HIGHLIGHTS

- Interesting Soviet architecture
- Huge arts and crafts store

INFORMATION

- ✚ G5
- ✉ 1000 Yan'an Zhonglu
- ☎ 6279 0279
- 🕐 Daily
- 🍴 Excellent restaurant on the premises
- 🚌 49, 71
- ♿ None
- 💵 Free
- ↔ Nanking Road (► 41), Children's Palace (► 31)
- ❓ Regular exhibitions

9

FRENCH CONCESSION

HIGHLIGHTS

- Fascinating architecture
- Excellent shopping and bars

INFORMATION

- ⊞ F6–J6
- ⊠ Main street—Huaihai Lu
- 🍴 Many excellent restaurants
- 🚇 Huaihai Lu
- 🚌 911, 42
- ♿ None
- ↔ Soong Qing-Ling's Residence (➤ 27), Site of First Communist Congress (➤ 37), Sun Yat Sen's Residence (➤ 35)

Detail: entrance of the Cercle Sportif Français

In the old days, if you wanted to assume a bohemian lifestyle and taste the high life, then you left the International Concession ruled by its Anglo-American obsession with business, and crossed the tracks to "Frenchtown."

France Outre Mer The French Concession lay to the south of the original British Settlement, and to the west of the old Chinese town. Having grown to an area of 3.9 square miles, it refused the invitation to join the Americans and British in forming the International Settlement in 1863. The French Settlement had its own buses and trams, its own electricity and its own judicial system and traffic regulations—and it added spice to the steaming cosmopolitan brew that was Shanghai. The French Concession attracted gangsters and revolutionaries, *bon-vivants* and refugees and by 1930 French residents were easily outnumbered by Americans, Britons and Russians.

Touring the French Concession The heart of the old concession was Avenue Joffre, today's Huaihai Lu, which even today is at least as good a shopping center as the more famous Nanking Road. Along here are a few reminders of the not-so-distant past—a prevalence of bakers selling European-style confections and the Red House Restaurant, formerly Chez Louis, once famous for its soufflé Grand Marnier. Fuxing Park, laid out in the Parisian style with wide paths flanked by trees, is one of the prettiest parks in the city. The Jin Jiang Hotel, built in 1931 as a private hotel for French residents and called Cathay Mansions, is where the Shanghai Communiqué was signed in 1972. Opposite is the grandiose entrance to the former French club, the Cercle Sportif Français, built before World War II.

10

SUN YAT SEN'S RESIDENCE

This small house in the French Concession is a reminder that Sun Yat Sen was the moving force behind the creation of a Chinese republic early in the 20th century. He lived here until his death in 1925.

Sun Yat Sen's revolution began China's modernization

Sun the revolutionary Sun Yat Sen was born close to Canton in 1866. He grew up as China tottered under the corrupt anachronism that was the Qing government and, although he was trained as a medical doctor, his real interest lay in political reform. Sun founded the "Revive China Society," which marked the beginning of serious republican agitation. Forced to flee abroad, he was kidnapped by the Qing authorities in London and held in the Chinese Legation. Intervention from the British Foreign Office led to his release, giving him all the publicity he required. But it was not until 1911 that his alliances with secret societies and elements in the Qing army bore fruit, as disturbances throughout China culminated in rebellion in Wuhan and the final overthrow of the last dynasty. Sun became president but the early years of the republic were difficult and, by his death in 1925, China remained in turmoil.

The residence Sun came to live in Shanghai in 1920 with his wife Soong Qing-Ling. Xiangshan Lu, in the former French Concession, was then Rue Molière. In this small house with an arcaded portico and a garden, Sun spent his time being courted by emissaries of the Soviet Union who were anxious to spread their brand of revolution to China. The house is supposed to be as it was during his life, simply furnished in a mixture of Western and Chinese styles with the addition of photographs and other reminders of the period.

HIGHLIGHTS

* Handsome period villa furnished as it was when lived in by Sun Yat Sen

INFORMATION

* H6
* 7 Xiangshan Lu
* 63589469
* Daily 9:30–11 and 2–4:30
* 24, 41
* Inexpensive
* French Concession (➤ 34), Site of First Communist Congress (➤ 37)

11

FLOWER & BIRD MARKET

One of the highlights of a visit to China is to wander through its markets. Tucked away in a narrow street close to the Nanking Road, Shanghai's Flower and Bird Market provides an entertaining glimpse of local life.

HIGHLIGHT

● Insight into daily Chinese life

INFORMATION

🞙 H5
✉ Jiangyin Lu
🕐 Daily, early until late
🍴 Snack stalls along the street
🚌 109
♿ None
💲 Free
↔ Nanking Road (➤ 41), Shanghai Museum (➤ 38)

Location Across the Nanking Road and a little way to the west of the Park Hotel is what is left of the old racecourse grandstand, distinguished by its clock tower. A street runs alongside and off this, to the right and easily missed, is a narrow lane almost entirely taken up with the Flower and Bird Market, which threads its way among small pre-war houses for about half a mile.

Fish and chops Despite the market's name, the main items for sale here seem to be fish, roots, teapots and "chops" (seals with the owner's personal signature). The Chinese love ornamental fish, and all the paraphernalia for their tanks. It is fascinating to see how browsers assess their potential purchases, looking for flaws probably only evident to the practised eye. You will also find wooden carvings, plants, snack stalls—and insects.

Customers spend a long time choosing their fish

Crickets In late summer, stallholders and itinerant vendors sell crickets in charming miniature baskets. Keeping and caring for crickets goes back to the Tang dynasty, while the sport of cricket fighting was cultivated in the Song era. Even now, although cricket fighting is outlawed, high prices are paid for the best fighters. Traditionally the crickets were kept in hollowed-out gourds, old examples of which fetch high prices. Nowadays people buy crickets for their "song."

First Communist Congress

It is a quirk of history that an attractive house in the French sector of capitalist Shanghai was one of the few safe places in China where early meetings of the Chinese Communist Party could be held.

History While a few intellectuals in China had dabbled in Marxism before, it was the Russian Revolution in 1917—coincidentally at a time of political turmoil in the infant Chinese republic—that highlighted Communism's possibilities. The Chinese were impressed that the Bolsheviks renounced some of the agreements extorted from the Chinese at the Treaty of Versailles.

Mao Mao Zedong, later to become the leader of the People's Republic of China, was a founder member of the Chinese Communist Party. Born in the village of Shaoshan in Hunan province, he had trained as a teacher but was led by his experience of rural poverty into the Communist movement. His master stroke was to establish, early on, a broad base among peasant farmers, rather than—as conventional Marxist doctrine dictated—among the urban proletariat.

The First Congress The word "congress" is a grand word for a meeting of 12 people who constituted the inaugural gathering of an organized Chinese Communist Party. But it is of course a sacred element in party mythology and so of importance in Chinese history. The dozen founding members, including Mao, met in July, 1921, at what was 106 Rue Wantz, a home of one of the delegates. The pleasing brick house with elegant carvings over the doorways is supposedly furnished as it was at the time, complete with ashtrays and teacups. An exhibition tells of the fates of the various delegates.

HIGHLIGHTS

- Insight into Chinese politics
- Interesting photographs

INFORMATION

- ✚ H6
- ✉ 374 Huangpi Nanlu
- ☎ 6328 1177
- 🕐 Daily
- 🍴 None
- 📅 12, 24
- ♿ None
- 💰 Inexpensive
- ↔ French Concession (▶ 34)

The delegates' Hall of Fame

13

SHANGHAI MUSEUM

One of the great museums of the world, it houses an unparalleled collection of bronzes, porcelain and scroll paintings. Don't miss it.

HIGHLIGHTS

- Paintings and ceramics
- Excellent presentation

INFORMATION

- ✚ J5
- ✉ 201 Renmin Square
- ☎ 6372 3500
- ◎ Daily 9–4
- 🍴 Good cafés (£/££) on premises
- 🚌 23, 49
- ♿ Few
- 💷 Moderate
- ↔ Nanking Road (➤ 41), Great World Center (➤ 40)
- ❓ Audio tours, high definition Graphics Hall

The new museum The original Shanghai Museum was established in 1952 in the old Horse Racing Club on the Nanking Road. In 1959, it was moved to Henan Road and located in the former Zhong Hui Bank, once owned by the powerful gangster Big-eared Du. In 1996, a new museum on People's Square, built especially to contain the collection of some 120,000 cultural relics, was opened to the public in 11 galleries and three exhibition halls. From the outside, it is the unique architectural style that catches the eye with a design consisting of a square base and a circular crown from which emanate four arch-like handles—the ensemble is supposed to represent a Han dynasty bronze mirror on an ancient bronze ding tripod (a food container).

Exhibits The excellent layout inside and the lighting displays the exhibits to their best advantage. Although there are a number of different themes, the three principal exhibitions are those of bronzes and stone sculpture on the ground floor, ceramics on the second floor, and paintings on the third floor. Other galleries are devoted to jade, Chinese coins, seals, calligraphy, traditional furniture, and the art of China's minority peoples. There are also cafeterias and two excellent shops.

The lighting and presentation here is beyond compare

INTERNATIONAL SETTLEMENT

Shanghai's atmosphere is best savored by strolling along the older streets of the International Settlement, which combines the elements of both old and new and demonstrates the true spirit of the city.

Much of the best of this historic city is being preserved

History After the Treaty of Nanking was signed in 1842, granting areas of Shanghai to foreign powers for trading purposes (concessions), the British were the first to establish their concession, extending from the Bund in the east to Xizang Zhonglu in the west and from Suzhou Creek in the north to Yan'an Lu in the south. The Americans, and other foreign nationals, apart from the French, established a concession in Hongkou, north of the creek. In 1863, the two merged to form the International Settlement, which by 1899 covered 8½ square miles. The International Settlement as an administrative entity is no more, but many of the buildings of the era remain.

Backstreets Sichuan Zhonglu, leading north from Nanjing Lu, will take you across Suzhou Creek to pass a large pre-war building with a huge clock, the principal post office of the city. Continuing further north from here you will come to Zhabei, heavily bombed during the early 1940s, but now a good area for cheap restaurants. No. 6 Jiujiang Lu was the site of the Louza Police Station, scene of the 1925 May 30 Incident (► 11). Where Fuzhou Lu, notorious for its brothels and opium dens, meets Henan Lu was the location of the International Settlement Municipal Council, the settlement's administrative headquarters. The Metropole Hotel, which in the 1930s offered the best meal in town, still stands at No. 180 Jiujiang Lu was the "Wall Street" of Shanghai—American Express was at No. 158, the Italian Bank at No. 186. These buildings are now general offices.

HIGHLIGHTS

- The untrodden streets of the area north of Suzhou Creek
- Fascinating European style buildings

INFORMATION

- G5–K5
- Various restaurants and cafés
- 37 along Nanjing Lu, 21 along Beijing Lu
- None
- Various
- Nanking Road (► 41), Bund (► 48), Huangpu River (► 50)

15

THE GREAT WORLD CENTER

HIGHLIGHTS

● A taste of old Shanghai
● Daredevil performances

INFORMATION

✚ J5
✉ 1 Xizang Nanlu
☎ 6326 3760
⏰ Daily, last ticket sold at 8:30PM
🍴 Snacks available
🚌 18, 23
♿ None
💲 Moderate
↔ Nanking Road (► 41), Shanghai Museum (► 38)
❓ Evening performances

Chinese opera—a great spectacle

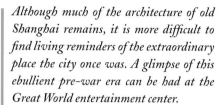

Although much of the architecture of old Shanghai remains, it is more difficult to find living reminders of the extraordinary place the city once was. A glimpse of this ebullient pre-war era can be had at the Great World entertainment center.

Shanghai nights On Xizang Nanlu, at the eastern end of People's Square, is a distinctive building, focused on a tapering tower of drums like a wedding cake. This is the Great World, an entertainment center designed in 1917 to encapsulate all that was strange and new in the world and to attract more money into this part of the French Concession. Inevitably it fell into the wrong hands—those of the gangster Huang Jinrong, alias Pockmarked Huang—and came to be known as "Rong's Great World." In the 1930s, movie director Josef von Sternberg visited it and saw sing-song girls (entertainers cum prostitutes), magicians, crickets in cages, pimps, midwives, earwax extractors, dried fish, tightrope walkers, marriage brokers, a stuffed whale, a mirror maze, modern toilets exposed and with instructions for their use—and much more.

The Great World today The government took over Great World in 1954 and recast it as the Palace of the Young Pioneers, where China's youth pursued healthy, ideologically sound pursuits. As Shanghai has regained some of its cosmopolitan flavor, so the Great World has returned to being an amusement center, albeit one considerably less salacious than the original. Nonetheless, it is worth visiting—apart from the various installed amusements, there are exciting performances, like motorcyclists on the Wall of Death, and an entertaining couple of hours can be spent here.

NANKING ROAD

Mention Shanghai to a Chinese and the chances are that he will immediately think of "Nanjing Lu," the Nanking Road. It has always represented the height of style and the best of shopping in China.

The past The name of Shanghai's most famous thoroughfare commemorates the treaty of the same name which, in 1842, gave trading rights to the foreign powers of the era. To the Chinese, it was the Great Maloo (or "horse road"). As Shanghai grew, so did the Nanking Road, snaking through the heart of the International Settlement to become, at its western end, the Bubbling Well Road (today's Nanjing Xilu), named after a well near the Jing'an Temple.

Today Although now rivalled by Huaihai Lu for shopping, Nanjing Lu remains the city's pre-eminent thoroughfare with the Bund and the Huangpu River at its eastern end. Nanjing Donglu (Nanking Road East), the most lively section, begins at the Peace Hotel and passes many shops, some dating from pre-World War II, others startlingly modern additions. Some, like the smaller food stores, and the calligraphy shop at 422 are of interest because of their traditional goods. Others, like the department stores near the intersection with Xizang Lu, are the new incarnations of old pre-war department stores. Where Nanjing Donglu meets Nanjing Xilu (Nanking Road West) is the old racecourse grandstand and clock, and the Park Hotel, the tallest building outside the Americas at the time of its construction in 1934.

HIGHLIGHTS

- Heart of workaday Shanghai
- Excellent shopping and period architecture

INFORMATION

- ✚ E5–K5
- 🍴 Many excellent restaurants
- Ⓢ Under construction
- 🚌 37
- ♿ None
- ↔ Peace Hotel (➤ 46), Flower and Bird Market (➤ 36)

The flavor of traditional China at the Art Store

41

17

YUYUAN (YU GARDEN)

HIGHLIGHTS

- Rockeries, bridges and pavilions
- Miniature fish-filled lake

INFORMATION

- K6
- 132 Anren Jie, Old Town
- Daily 8:30–4:30
- Plenty of restaurants nearby, in the Old Town
- 11, 126
- None
- Moderate
- French Concession (▶ 34), Shanghai Museum (▶ 38), Old Town (▶ 43), Huxingting Tea House (▶ 44)

Miniature lakes and fish bring life to the garden

Shanghai does have its surprises. Concealed from casual observation in the heart of the Old Town is one of the finest classical gardens remaining in China.

The Pan family The Yuyuan, or Yu Garden, has a very long history. In its current incarnation, it was created in the mid-16th century by a certain Pan Yunduan as an act of filial affection for his father. Pan, a native of Shanghai who had been in public service in Sichuan Province, must have been a wealthy and influential figure in the city, for the garden takes up almost 12 acres, a large chunk of the Old Town. By the time it was completed in 1577, however, Pan's father had died, and although additions were made to the garden from time to time, it suffered from neglect. Twice in the 19th century it was used as headquarters—in 1842 by the British Land Force led by Lieutenant-General Gough and in the 1850s by the Small Swords Society, dedicated to the restoration of the Ming dynasty.

Today's garden The Yuyuan exemplifies the classic Ming garden, where rock gardens, bridges and ponds surround pavilions and corridors to create an illusion of a natural landscape. In reality, although the materials used are the work of nature, the design is very obviously the work of man. But what is important in this garden is the "harmony of scale," its beauty lying in the intricate design which in the past would have permitted tranquil contemplation in a comparatively small area. An unusual feature is the sculpted dragon that curls around the top of the garden wall.

OLD TOWN

One of the unexpected pleasures of Shanghai is to discover—amid the high-rise modernity, an old Chinese town—the original Shanghai. In its narrow streets, you absorb something of the atmosphere and bustle of traditional China.

A worshipper at Chenxiangge Temple

History Until 1842 and the Treaty of Nanking, Shanghai was a walled town of moderate importance, concentrated in the area now called Nanshi. The walls were pulled down in 1911 in order to provide better access for stores and traders, but even now the area is self-contained and the route of the old walls can be traced along what are now Renmin Lu and Zhonghua Lu. You will still find a single wide street with a number of narrow alleys branching from it. The center of the town was dominated then, as it is today, by the Huxingting Tea House (➤ 44), the Yu Garden (➤ 42) and the Chenghuang Miao, or Temple of the City God (➤ 17).

Today Although there have been many changes, with the addition of new stores designed in the traditional Chinese style, the old Chinese town retains its pre-war atmosphere. There is a large number of small stores which specialize in items such as tea, walking sticks and even wigs. The newer stores sell jewelry and antiques. Perhaps the most enjoyable pastime is to patronize one of the several restaurants selling delicious freshly-made dumplings. The two principal entrances to the town are from Fuyou Lu, beside the Lao Fandian Restaurant (➤ 64), and through the arch of the Temple of the City God, off Fangbang Zhonglu. Once you are inside, any lane will eventually bring you to the central area, anchored by the Huxingting Tea House.

HIGHLIGHTS

- A hint of the atmosphere of old China
- Excellent snack food and stores

INFORMATION

- ✚ K6–K7
- 🍴 Plenty of restaurants in the area
- 🚌 11, 14, 26
- ♿ None
- 🎫 Free
- ↔ French Concession (➤ 34), Shanghai Museum (➤ 38)

19

HUXINGTING TEA HOUSE

The delightful old tea house, in its watery setting in the center of a lake, is the focal point of the Old Town. It fits in exactly with the China of popular imagination, a China that has all but disappeared.

Tea is still served in the traditional manner here

HIGHLIGHTS

- Charming building in entertaining location
- Cooling and restful on hot days

INFORMATION

- K6
- Old Town
- 6373 6950
- Daily upstairs 8:45AM–10PM and downstairs 5:30–10
- Plenty of restaurants near by, in the Old Town
- 11, 126
- None
- Moderate
- French Concession (► 34), Shanghai Museum (► 38), Old Town (► 43),
- Tea ceremony performed in the evening

Tea drinking Tea is widely produced throughout central and southern China and is also widely consumed in everyday life—taxi drivers often keep a jar with them, half filled with leaves to which boiling water is added throughout the day. There will probably be tea in your hotel room, and when people meet, or at an official function, tea will certainly be served at some point. In the past, however, every town had several tea houses, where conversation was an adjunct to an appreciation of good teas. However, an appreciation of fine teas and the art of tea drinking in its ceremonial form, where such matters as the quality of the water used are much considered, has largely vanished.

Huxingting The Huxingting Tea House, which sits surrounded by a small lake (and is sometimes known as the Mid-Lake Pavilion), is truly the center of the Old Town. Its precise origins are not entirely clear, but it probably dates from the 18th century and was originally part of both the Temple of the City God (► 17) and the Yu Garden. Eventually, as Shanghai prospered, parts of the garden, including the Tea House, were purchased by local merchants who used it as a meeting place for conducting business. A building of great charm, it is approached via the Nine Zig-Zag Bridge (shaped thus to throw off pursuing devils), over waters glittering with shoals of goldfish. Inside you may drink good quality tea from traditional teapots—surprisingly refreshing on hot summer days.

SHANGHAI FRIENDSHIP STORE

Shanghai has become a giant emporium with a choice of shopping that can be bewildering if you don't have much time to spend. The Friendship Store is the most convenient choice when you're looking for essential souvenirs.

Why The Friendship Store? When China first started to encourage foreign visitors in the late 1970s, there was almost nowhere to buy souvenirs, or anything else. Local stores had been rendered practically obsolete by the extreme austerity of the Cultural Revolution, and in any case there were no quality goods to fill their shelves. At the same time, China was operating a dual currency system—ordinary currency (as used by everyone now) and exchange certificates, representing foreign currency, for foreigners. Special "Friendship Stores" were created where only exchange certificates could be used and only foreigners could shop. Here the best of Chinese goods were available, along with imported items for the expatriate community.

Reliability Today there are so many stores and markets in China, selling a variety of goods, that Friendship Stores might be thought to have become an irrelevance. Yet these government emporiums continue to play an important role. It is too soon for many home-grown Shanghai stores to have established a reputation for reliability or excellence, so a huge store like the Friendship Store, where everything comes with a government seal of approval, from antiques to silks, arts and crafts, jewelry, and books, still has its place. Its excellent location, conveniently close to the Bund, means that it is easy to find and on its well-stocked five floors you would be unlucky not to find something to suit.

HIGHLIGHTS

- Several floors of concentrated shopping
- Not many bargains but guarantee of quality and authenticity

INFORMATION

- L5
- 40 Beijing Donglu
- 6323 1419
- Daily 9AM–10PM
- Café (S/SS), restaurant (SS/SSS) on premises
- 22, 26, 37
- None
- Free to enter
- Nanking Road (► 41), Bund (► 48), Huangpu River (► 50)

Chinese opera mask

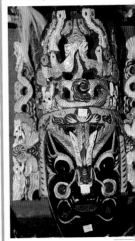

PEACE HOTEL

HIGHLIGHTS

- Classic art-deco architecture
- Jazz in the evening

INFORMATION

- K5
- 20 Nanjing Donglu
- 6321 6888
- Daily
- Café (S/SS), bar (SS), restaurant (SS/SSS) on premises
- 126, 37, 42, 55
- None
- Free but very expensive to stay there
- Nanking Road (➤ 41), Bund (➤ 48), Huangpu River (➤ 50),
- Jazz band performs in the evening

The hotel is a landmark

Even if you don't stay at the Peace Hotel, you should drop in one evening to have a drink and to hear its famous jazz band. This relic from Shanghai's extravagant past is one of the city's symbols.

The Sassoons Of the many families of Sephardic Jews that flourished in pre-war Shanghai, the best known is the Sassoon family. They originally fled an intolerant Baghdad in the 18th century to make a fortune in Bombay and then proceeded to buy wharf space and warehouses in Shanghai. Successive generations of Sassoons invested in the port, but it was Victor (later Sir Victor) Sassoon who built the well-known landmark on the Bund, now known as the Peace Hotel. Though it represents the hated era of foreign domination in the guise of the Sassoons, many new skyscrapers ape its distinctive pyramidical roof design.

The Cathay There had been a Sassoon House on the Bund for some time, but Victor Sassoon had visions of a skyscraper as a modern headquarters for his business empire and wanted to include a fabulous hotel into the bargain. Today's Peace Hotel, originally the Cathay, dates from 1930, with art-deco ironwork and high ceilings inside and looking somewhat like a smaller Empire State Building outside. The ground floor and the next three above it were reserved for offices. The remainder were taken up by what Victor hoped would be the finest hotel in the East. It had all the best in technology and service that the period could offer, while the Horse & Hounds Bar became the most fashionable rendezvous in the city. The hotel attracted the rich and famous including no less than Noel Coward. Today the Peace Hotel incorporates the old Palace Hotel from across the Nanking Road.

LU XUN PARK (HONGKOU PARK)

If you want a window on Shanghai life away from the city center, then try to get to Lu Xun Park, where local people come to find refuge and meet friends away from their crowded housing conditions.

Hongkou Hongkou is the area north of Suzhou Creek (the Wusong River), a large part of which was the former American Concession before it merged with the British Concession in 1863 to become the International Settlement. The accepted date of its foundation is 1848 when a church mission was established here. An American Consulate soon followed but was later moved to a more central area, while Hongkou became home to many Japanese, earning the soubriquet of Little Tokyo. It was also the residence of the Mixed Court (administered jointly by a Chinese magistrate and a foreign assessor) as well as to several dairies, the Russian post office and various risqué cabarets.

Lu Xun Lu Xun Park, originally laid out in 1905, has a large lake with rowboats for rent in the summer. Shrubs and flowers attract butterflies, while the open air setting draws amateur painters and opera singers. Every fall, there are chrysanthemum shows. Above all, the park is known for its associations with the eminent writer Lu Xun, who lived in Hongkou from 1927 until his death in 1936, and is best known for *The True Story of Ah Q* whch lampoons the Chinese character. He was also influential in the simplification of Chinese script. His house, at 9 Dalu Xinchun, Sanyin Lu, is open to the public and provides an opportunity to see housing in what was the Japanese part of Shanghai. In the park, there is a also a museum dedicated to Lu Xun's life, as well as his mausoleum and his likeness cast in bronze.

Relaxing in the winter sun in Hongkou Park

HIGHLIGHTS

- Lu Xun's mausoleum and Memorial Hall
- Boating lake

INFORMATION

- ⊞ L1
- ✉ 146 Jiangwan Lu
- 🕐 Daily 6AM–8PM
- 🍴 Snacks sold at stalls in the park
- 🚌 9, 18, 21
- ♿ None
- 💷 Inexpensive
- ↔ International Settlement (▶ 39)

23

THE BUND

HIGHLIGHTS

- Panoramic views
- Waterfront European style buildings

INFORMATION

- K5–L5
- Zhongshan Donglu
- Always
- Various restaurants and cafés
- 42, 55, 65
- None
- Various
- International Settlement (➤ 39), Huangpu River (➤ 50), Nanking Road (➤ 41)

Early morning waltzing on the Bund

Traveling by ship from Europe or America in the 1930s, the expatriate's first view of Shanghai would have been the waterfront street known as the Bund, a grand slice of the colonial world that is still impressive today.

Waitan The Bund (a word of Anglo-Indian origin, meaning "waterfront" or "embankment") is now known as Waitan or Zhongshan Donglu and runs along the Huangpu River from Suzhou Creek in the north to Yan'an Lu in the south. The buildings that line it date from the early 20th century and are entirely Western in style. The Bund is where modern Shanghai began and it remains the hub of the city.

The buildings Although changes have been made—the trams have gone, as have the old "go-downs," or warehouses, and statues of foreigners —the Bund would be instantly recognizable to a 1930s resident. A walk from south to north would begin with the Shanghai Club at No. 3 (now the Dong Fang Hotel), which claimed to have the longest bar in the world. The bar no longer exists in its entirety. The domed building at No. 12 was the Hong Kong & Shanghai Bank, built in 1921. Next door, surmounted by a clock once known as Big Ching, is the Customs House of 1927 with beautiful ceiling mosaics inside. Next to the main building of the Peace Hotel on the corner of Nanking Road is the Bank of China (1934). No. 27 was the headquarters of Jardine Matheson, one of the early companies to prosper from the opium trade, while No. 32 was the old British Consulate.

ORIENTAL PEARL TV TOWER

Only a few years ago, the tallest building in Shanghai—indeed in China—was still the Park Hotel on the Nanking Road. Now it has been dwarfed by many others, above all by the new TV Tower, which an unequalled view of the city.

Pudong New Area Pudong, the area across the Huangpu River from the Bund, is the fastest growing urban area in the world, already as large as Shanghai itself. Until the early 1990s, it was full of rundown factories and offices and farmland, accessible only by ferry. The only reason to go there would have been for the view across the river to the Bund (if you could find an opening before an official drove you back to the city proper). Now Pudong is a Special Economic Zone. The old buildings have been replaced by skyscrapers, streets have been built, and the area is linked to the city center by tunnel and bridge.

Oriental TV Tower Pudong still has little to offer, except insofar as it exemplifies a China that is modernizing and changing before one's eyes. There is, however, still the view back across the river to the Bund and the giant Oriental Pearl TV Tower, not a building of great beauty but currently the tallest building in Asia and the third in the world (at press time, that is). Its top truly disappears into the clouds and in fine weather, the panorama over Shanghai and beyond, from a viewing area half-way up, is splendid. The tower is 1,245 feet high and in 1995 began broadcasting programs through nine television channels and ten FM channels. To the Chinese it is known as "two dragons playing with a pearl," reflecting the Chinese way of describing things in fanciful ways. There is a souvenir store on the viewing platform and a café and jazz band on the first floor.

HIGHLIGHTS

- Wonderful views across the city
- A glimpse into the future of Shanghai

INFORMATION

- L5
- Pudong Park, Yantai Lu
- 5879 8888
- 8AM—9PM
- Ferry from opposite Yan'an Donglu
- None
- Expensive
- Nanking Road (▶ 41), Friendship Store (▶ 45), Bund (▶ 48), International Settlement (▶ 39)
- Jazz band in café

New Pudong skyline

HUANGPU RIVER/YANGTSE RIVER

HIGHLIGHTS

- The busy port
- Confluence with the mighty Yangtse

INFORMATION

- ✚ F10–N5
- ✉ Boat leaves from Bund pier, close to Huangpu Park
- ☎ 6374 4461
- 🎫 Cruises usually leave at 10:45AM, 2PM and 7PM daily
- 🍴 Bar on board ship
- 🚌 42, 55, 65
- ♿ None
- 💷 Moderate—tickets through CITS or from a kiosk close to the pier
- ↔ Nanking Road (▶ 41), Friendship Store (▶ 45), Bund (▶ 48), International Settlement (▶ 39)
- ❓ Performances often given on river cruise

An uncharacteristically empty Huangpu River

The Huangpu and Yangtse rivers are the original reasons for Shanghai's prosperity. A river cruise along the Huangpu will demonstrate the importance of the two waterways, as well as showing aspects of this huge city you might not otherwise see.

Two rivers The Yangtse is the longest river in China. Rising in the Tibetan Plateau, it meanders right across the country, passing through several provinces, and most famously, the Three Gorges (▶ 22–3). The Huangpu, only 70 miles in length, runs from Lake Tai and empties into the Yangtse River some 17 miles downstream. Its average width through the city is 440 yards and its average depth 27 feet. Large ships were able to enter the wide mouth of the Yangtse, make the short journey along the deep channel of the Huangpu and unload their cargoes at the wharves along the Bund. The goods were transported by barges along Suzhou Creek and then along the network of canals for distribution throughout China.

Touring the Huangpu Boat tours leave every afternoon (and in the evening in summer) from the Bund, a little way north of the Peace Hotel. If you travel first class, the journey is very comfortable. Refreshments are provided and, during the return journey, there is often a performance of some kind, usually magic or acrobatics. You first pass Suzhou Creek on the left, overlooked by Shanghai Mansions, and then the International Passenger Terminal, while to your right is Pudong (▶ 49). Then comes the Yangshupu Power Plant and Fuxing Island, where Chiang Kai Shek made his last stand before fleeing to Taiwan. Finally you meet the Yangtse, before returning to the city.

SHANGHAI's *best*

ARCHITECTURE

See Top 25 Sights for
CHILDREN'S PALACE (▶ 31)
GREAT WORLD CENTER (▶ 40)
PEACE HOTEL (▶ 46)

1950s survivor

The long years of anti-Western ideology have had unexpected benefits in Shanghai. Renovations that began in 1997 in the old Hong Kong & Shanghai Bank on the Bund revealed a set of beautiful mosaics painted over in the 1950s.

DONG HU HOTEL

One of the villas (No. 7) that comprise this art deco hotel once belonged to the infamous pre-war gangster, Du Yuesheng (▶ 12). The other villas belonged to wealthy foreigners.

🔢 F6 ✉ 70 Donghu Lu ☎ 6415 8158 🕐 Daily 🍴 Restaurants 🚌 49 ♿ None 🆓 Free

THE GOLDEN CAGE

Formerly a bank, this building at the intersection of Sichuan Lu and Guangdong Lu was once the home of the concubines of a Shanghai character called Yu Aqing, hence its nickname "the Golden Cage." Beautiful stained glass and magnificent ceiling mosaics.

🔢 K5 ✉ 93 Guangdong Lu 🚌 17

HENGSHAN HOTEL

The former Picardie Mansions was once an apartment block for well-to-do expatriates in the French Concession.

🔢 D7 ✉ 534 Hengshan Lu ☎ 6437 7050 🕐 Daily 🍴 Restaurants 🚇 Xujiahui 🚌 42 ♿ None 🆓 Free

European legacy

The single most interesting aspect of Shanghai is the Western architecture left over from its period of foreign domination before 1949. There is perhaps more European art deco and art nouveau architecture in Shanghai than anywhere else in the world.

MARSHALL HOUSE

Between 1945 and 1949 this splendid French Concession mansion built in 1920 by a French nobleman, was the home of U.S. General George Marshall, chief mediator between Mao and Chiang Kai Shek. It is now a small hotel.

🔢 F7 ✉ 160 Taiyuan Lu 🚌 42 ♿ None 🆓 Free

METROPOLE HOTEL

This miniature skyscraper, also a hotel, was famous for its restaurants before 1945. This is where Soong Mei-Ling and Chiang Kai Shek had their wedding banquet.

🔢 K5 ✉ 180 Jiangxi Zhonglu ☎ 6321 3030 🕐 Daily 🍴 Restaurants 🚌 49 ♿ None 🆓 Free

MOLLER HOUSE

A classic piece of Shanghai architecture—a curious concoction of Gothic towers and spires that looks as if it might suit Count Dracula. It was the home of a Scandinavian shipping magnate—now it is the headquarters of the Communist Youth League and can be seen only from the road.

🔢 G6 ✉ 30 Shanxi Nanlu 🚌 42

MORRISS VILLAS

This cluster of four villas in what was a handsome garden was originally owned by the proprietor of the *North China Daily News*, the old Shanghai daily newspaper. He died in the gatehouse shortly after the arrival of the Communists. It is now Ruijing Hotel.

➕ G7 ✉ 118 Ruijin 2-Lu ☎ 6472 5222 🚌 41

PUJIANG HOTEL

Now a budget hotel, this building just across the bridge at the northern end of the Bund, opposite the Russian Consulate, was formerly the Astor, one of the one of the finest hotels in the city.

➕ L4 ✉ 15 Huangpu Lu ☎ 6324 6388 🕐 Daily 🍴 Restaurants 🚌 28 ♿ None 💵 Free

SASSOON VILLA

Sir Victor Sassoon (▶ 46) was one of Shanghai's most eminent tycoons. He lived in the Peace Hotel but also built this mock-Tudor country estate, where he gave lavish parties in a drawing-room complete with minstrel gallery and massive fireplace. It is now a guest house in the grounds of the Cypress Hotel.

➕ D7 ✉ 2419 Hongqiao Lu ☎ 6268 8868 🕐 Daily 🍴 Restaurants 🚌 57 ♿ None 💵 Free

SHANGHAI ARTS & CRAFTS RESEARCH INSTITUTE

This institution, devoted to the practice of, and research into, traditional Chinese arts and crafts, occupies an elegant mansion, with fine stucco work and a beautiful garden. It belonged to a French general before becoming the residence of Chen Yi, a former mayor.

➕ F6 ✉ 79 Fenyang Lu 🕐 Daily 8:30–4:30 🚌 42 ♿ None 💵 Cheap

XUHUI DISTRICT

An area in the southwest of Shanghai of houses and villas in Central European style, with ocher-colored tiles and shuttered windows.

➕ E7 ✉ Hengshan Lu/Wuxing Lu 🍴 Restaurants 🚌 42 ♿ None 🚇 Free

Competition

The story goes that there was tremendous competition in the 1930s between Victor Sassoon, proprietor of the Peace Hotel, and H.H. Kung, director of the Bank of China, to construct the city's tallest building. Sassoon probably won, but even now it is hard to know whether the hotel or the bank building is the taller.

Old colonial architecture of Shanghai

CHURCHES & TEMPLES

See Top 25 Sights for:
JADE BUDDHA TEMPLE (➤ 32)
LONGHUA TEMPLE & PAGODA (➤ 30)
XUJIAHUI CATHEDRAL (➤ 26)

Synagogues

Considering that there was once an extensive and influential Jewish community in Shanghai, it is surprising to discover that there is no surviving synagogue in the city. Silas Hardoon built one of the most interesting examples, the lower portion of which survives as a factory on Huqiu Lu, the former Museum Street.

CONFUCIAN TEMPLE (WEN MIAO)

This Confucian Temple is to be found in the Old (Chinese) Town, to the south of the Temple of the City God and close to the site of the old West Gate. As well as the temple dedicated to Confucius, there is a small market and swings for children.

➕ J7 ✉ Wenmiao Lu 🕐 Daily 🚇 11 ♿ None 💶 Inexpensive

JING'AN TEMPLE

The western part of Nanjing Lu was known as Bubbling Well Road until 1949. Before that, it was Jing'an Road, named after this temple (the name means Temple of Tranquillity) which has stood on the site for over 1,700 years. During the early part of the 20th century, it was the richest temple in the city, headed by Abbot Khi Vehdu, who doubled as a gangster—in public, and in the company of his various concubines, he was protected by White Russian guards. The current buildings, which date from the Ming (1368–1644) and Qing (1644–1912) dynasties, were restored in 1984 and there are over 50 Buddhist monks resident here. Inside is a bell cast from 3½ tons of copper in 1183.

➕ F5 ✉ 1686 Nanjing Xilu 🕐 Daily 🚇 20, 37 ♿ None 💶 Inexpensive

MUEN INTERDENOMINATIONAL CHURCH

A short way south of the Nanking Road you will find this large church, which caters to the surprisingly substantial Christian congregation, of about 3,000, in the center of Shanghai. The church dates back to the 1920s, is run by a Chinese woman pastor and has played host to evangelist Billy Graham in 1988.

➕ J5 ✉ 316 Xizang Zhonglu 🕐 Daily 🚇 18 ♿ None 💶 Free

Places of worship

Because of the cosmopolitan nature of its pre-war history, Shanghai has, for a city in an officially atheistic country, an unusual number of places of worship, many of which have been renovated.

RUSSIAN ORTHODOX CHURCHES

There are a couple of former Russian Orthodox churches in Shanghai, which once catered to the large population of refugees from the 1917 Revolution. With their distinctive onion domes, both lie within the former French Concession. Neither serves its original function—they are now warehouses.

➕ GH6 and FG6 ✉ Gaolan Lu and Xinle Lu 🚇 45, 126

SHINTO SHRINE

This little temple, now a coffee bar, is in an area once largely populated by Japanese, Zhapei, to the north of Suzhou Creek. The shrine, named for the Japanese religion, is on the left as you walk north along Zhapu Lu, at a point where the restaurants—of which there are many here—come to an end. The temple/coffee bar, was used as a resting place for the ashes of dead Japanese soldiers before they were sent home.

✚ L4 ✉ Zhapu Lu ⏰ Daily 🍴 Restaurant 🚌 25, 65 ♿ None
✋ Free

WHITE CLOUD TEMPLE (BAI YUN SI)

This Taoist temple built in 1883 lies outside the west gate in the Old Town on Fangxie Lu. It is the birthplace of the Quanzhen Sect of Taoism. Inside, a statue of the Jade Emperor is the object of worshippers' veneration. Regular ceremonies are accompanied by traditional Tao music using gongs and flutes.

✚ J7 ✉ No 8, Lane 100, Xilin Houlu ⏰ Daily 🚌 43 ♿ None
✋ Inexpensive

Power union

To the north of Suzhou Creek, on Kunshan Lu, off Sichuan Beilu, is the Kunshan Protestant church where Chiang Kai Shek was married to Soong Mei-Ling.

Decorative arch in the Jing'an Temple

MARKETS

See Top 25 Sights for:
FLOWER AND BIRD MARKET (► 36)

Haggling

When you are haggling in the markets and you want to point out that the price asked is too high, you can say *"tai gui le"* (pronounced *"tie gway ler"*), which means "too expensive." *Caveat emptor* is always a useful maxim when shopping for antiques in China.

DONGTAI MARKET

This market is favored by owners of antiques stores and expatriates who live in the city. The 200 or so stalls are open for business daily and deal in ceramics, gold ornaments, stoneware and antiques along with flowers, birds, fish, and insects.

✚ J6–7 ✉ Liuhe Lu ⊙ Daily ∏ Restaurants ⊟ 23 ⓖ None ✋ Free

FUYOU MARKET

The most famous market for antiques in Shanghai takes place on a Sunday just outside the Old Town. Until 1998, several dozen mobile stalls lined Fuyou Lu to provide the largest antiques market in the city—many of the stallholders would arrive before dawn to insure a good position along the road. Now the market has a permanent home on Fangbang Zhonglu, close to Henan Nanlu. Prices can be very high here, so haggling is a must.

✚ K6 ✉ Fangbang Zhonglu ⊙ Daily ∏ Restaurants ⊟ 66 ⓖ None ✋ Free

Careful hunting can turn up some good bargains at antiques markets

HUA BAO LOU

The market is held in the basement of one of the buildings on the edge of the central area of the Old Town. There is a large number of stalls selling antiques and bric-à-brac, but prices are high and the stallholders are not always inclined to volunteer important information—for example that a perfect piece of "Ming porcelain" is actually a reproduction.

✚ K6 ✉ Fangbanglu 🕐 Daily 🍴 Restaurants 🚌 11, 66
♿ None ✋ Free

LIUHE ANTIQUES MARKET

This is perhaps the most reliable market in Shanghai to buy antiques. Located west of the Old Town, it consists of two streets of stalls selling antiques and bric-à-brac, and stores specializing in old radios, old clocks, antique furniture, and so on. The market has a good reputation, but keep an eye open for reproductions.

✚ J6 ✉ Liuhekou Lu 🕐 Daily 🍴 Restaurants 🚌 17, 18, 23 ♿ None ✋ Free

TOY MARKET (➤ 62)

ZHAOJIABIN OLD COINS AND STAMP MARKET

As the name suggests, this market is primarily aimed at collectors. Here you can sell as well as buy and trade.

✚ F7 ✉ Intersection of Taiyuan Lu and Zhaojiabin 🕐 Check with CITS 🍴 Restaurants 🚌 42 ♿ None ✋ Free

An advertising poster from pre-war Shanghai

ZHONGHUA XIN FLEA MARKET

The largest market in Shanghai is made up of private traders with permanent stores that are open for business every day, selling antiques, bicycle parts, electronic goods and all types of bric-à-brac.

✚ H2–K2 ✉ Zhonghua Xinlu 🕐 Daily 🍴 Restaurants 🚌 65 ♿ None ✋ Free

Markets

Although most markets claim to specialize, they all sell what they can. Among the old or antique objects you are likely to see are opium devices, furniture, statues of Buddha, lamps, pocket watches, radios, pre-war advertising material and items from the Cultural Revolution.

PARKS

See Top 25 Sights for:
LU XUN PARK (► 47)

The tranquil lake at Hongkou Park (► 47)

The bishop's seat

Today's Zhongshan Park, off Changning Lu in the west of the city, was formerly Jessfield Park, seat of the Bishop of Shanghai. It was named after a Chinese orphan who was adopted by a Portuguese resident and educated in America and who later married her benefactor.

FUXING PARK

This was formerly a private garden which, in 1908, was purchased by the French residents and turned into a park in the Parisian style, with wide walkways bounded by trees. It is a pleasant and tranquil spot for a stroll.

➕ H6 ✉ Fuxing Zhonglu 🕐 Daily 🍴 Restaurants 🚌 24 ♿ None 🎟 Free

GUANGQI PARK

A small park close to Xujiahui Cathedral holds the tomb of Xu Guangqi, one of the earliest converts of the Italian Jesuit missionary, Matteo Ricci. It was Xu who bequeathed the land to the Jesuits for the construction of the church.

➕ D8 ✉ Nandan Lu 🕐 Daily 🚌 89 ♿ None 🎟 Free

GUILIN PARK

Tucked away in the industrial suburbs in the south-western part of the city, this is an attractive park in Suzhou style, with rock gardens and pools laid out to create artificial scenes, in grounds once owned by the gangster Pockmarked Huang (► 12).

➕ A10 ✉ Guilin Lu 🕐 Daily 🍴 Restaurants 🚌 43 ♿ None 🎟 Inexpensive

HUANGPU PARK
Located at the northern end of the Bund near the bridge, this is the infamous park where a notice was said to forbid entry to "Dogs and Chinese" (the wording was not exactly like that in fact) (► panel this page). It is a pleasant park overlooking the river, with an ugly monument, beneath which is the small Huangpu Park Museum with exhibits about old Shanghai.
L5 The Bund Daily Restaurants 65 None Free

JING'AN PARK
Opposite the Jing'an Temple is the Jing'an Park which covers what used to be the Bubbling Well Cemetery. There is a tea house and a small pavilion with fluted columns in a classical style.
F5 Nanjing Xilu Daily Restaurants 20, 37 None Inexpensive

PUDONG PARK
This new park forms part of the "New Bund" on the east bank of the Huangpu. The park is a refreshing contrast to the relentless business landscape of the Special Economic Zone of Pudong. It is dominated by the Oriental Pearl TV Tower (► 49), and of course there are fine views across the river towards the old Bund.
L5 Yantai Lu Daily Restaurants Ferry None Inexpensive

RENMIN PARK
The People's Park, opposite the Park Hotel, has been created out of what was once the racetrack. It's a good place to get some fresh air away from the crowds and stores on Nanking Road.
J5 Nanjing Xilu Daily 20, 37 None Inexpensive

XIANGYANG PARK
A delightful little park, once a private garden, with the silhouette of a Russian Orthodox Church behind it. It is especially pretty in spring when the cherry trees are in blossom.
G6 Huaihai Zhonglu Daily 911, 42 None Inexpensive

Parks and the Chinese

Until the late 1920s, parks were largely the preserve of the foreign community. After the Nationalists came to power in 1928, most gardens were opened to the Chinese and between June and December there were 675,602 visitors to the Public Gardens on the Bund alone.

Monk at the Jing'an Temple on the Nanking Road

PLACES TO WATCH THE CITY

See Top 25 Sights for:
ORIENTAL PEARL TV TOWER (▶ 49)

Shanghai by night

The rooftop terrace of the Peace Hotel is sometimes open in summer. Eating up there on a sultry night is an atmospheric experience enhanced by good views of the Huangpu River and the lights on Nanking Road.

NEW WORLD

At the intersection of Nanking and Xizang roads is one of several department stores that have been refurbished to deal with the demands of the newly monied Shanghainese. With frequent demonstrations of new products, it is a good place to see the locals at earnest play.

➕ J5 ✉ Nanjing Xilu ⏰ Daily 🍴 Restaurants 🚌 20, 37 ♿ None 🎟 Free

OCEAN HOTEL

The revolving restaurant atop this hotel in Hongkou, north of Suzhou Creek, has magnificent views of the Bund, the Huangpu River and the entire Hongkou area.

➕ N4 ✉ 1171 Dongdaming Lu ☎ 6545 8888 ⏰ Daily 🍴 Restaurants 🚌 28 ♿ None 🎟 Free

PARK HOTEL RESTAURANT

The restaurants on the upper floors of the Park Hotel, once the tallest building in China, offer a good view of the city, especially down the Nanking Road towards the Bund.

➕ J5 ✉ 170 Nanjing Xilu ☎ 6327 5225 ⏰ Daily 🍴 Restaurants 🚌 20, 37 ♿ None 🎟 Free

Shanghai Lanes, where you will see a less glamorous Shanghai

SHANGHAI LANES

Off the main streets are the former Shanghai Lanes, areas in the former concessions where the Chinese lived then and still live today. Narrow, packed streets and alleys lined with period houses, they are excellent places for exploring local life. There are areas north of Nanjing Xilu, in the Jing'an District, north of Beijing Lu, and in Hongkou.

➕ J4, F4, L4 ♿ None 🎟 Free

SHANGHAI-STYLE DISHES

SHANGHAI-STYLE
Shanghai cuisine belongs to the eastern, or Yangzhou, school of Chinese cooking, which embraces the cooking of Suzhou, Hangzhou, and Nanking. Although this style of cooking is sometimes called "Shanghai food," it is a misnomer because although Shanghai cuisine is known for its sweetness, it has its own specialties.

DAZHA CRAB
This famous—and expensive—crab dish is only available between October and December. The crab is served whole with a light sauce.

DRUNKEN CHICKEN
A whole chicken is cooked and then soaked overnight in Shaoxing wine, a rice wine not unlike Madeira. It is then stir-fried before serving.

Shanghai-style snacks in relaxing surroundings

DUMPLINGS
Small restaurants selling dumplings abound in Shanghai. Some dumplings are filled with meat or vegetables, others with red bean sauce, and still others with a sweet paste flavored with the osmanthus flower and sesame and served in a bowl of hot water. *Luo buo ci bin* is a delicious pastry stuffed with onion. Another delicacy is sticky rice wrapped in lotus leaf.

RED-STEWED FISH
Carp is boiled and then soused in a sweet vinegar-like brown sauce.

SMOKED FISH
A grass carp is cut into small, thin pieces which are marinated for several hours in a mixture of ginger juice, Shaoxing wine, soy sauce and scallions. Then the fish pieces are quickly fried and while at their hottest immersed in a syrup containing five-spice powder. Eaten cold (to ensure that all the syrup has been absorbed) the fish has a smoky taste.

STIR-FRIED FRESH EELS
For this delicious dish, locally caught baby eels are quickly fried and then covered in boiling oil and finely ground white pepper.

French fries
Shanghai is perhaps the only place in China where French fries might be served as part of a Chinese meal, one of the few instances where Western food has made an impact on Chinese cooking.

61

ATTRACTIONS FOR CHILDREN

Shanghai Zoo is popular with children

Chinese and children

The Chinese love children and it is widely believed that they tend to spoil them, especially nowadays as the "one child policy" has denied many people a traditional family life. Only children are known as "*xiao huangdi,*" or "little emperors."

See Top 25 Sights for:
GREAT WORLD CENTER (➤ 40)

ACROBATS
Shanghai is famous for the Shanghai Acrobatic Troupe and a performance is given nearly every day in the old Lyceum Theater. Although a few animal acts have been introduced, the program consists mainly of breathtaking acrobatics.
🚇 G6 ☒ Maoming Nanlu/Changle Lu ☎ 253 0788 ⏰ Daily 🍴 Restaurants 🚌 41 ♿ None 💷 Moderate

ARTS & CRAFTS RESEARCH INSTITUTE
This beautiful old mansion in the former French Concession provides an opportunity to see how some of China's crafts are made. The institute specializes in painting, paper-cutting, carving and dough-figurine modeling.
🚇 F6 ☒ 79 Fengyang Lu ☎ 6437 7050 ⏰ Daily 8:30–4:30 🚌 96 ♿ None 💷 Inexpensive

SHANGHAI MUSEUM OF NATURAL HISTORY
This centrally located museum has an interesting collection of items relating to Chinese flora and fauna. There are stuffed animals, photographs and, especially popular with children, dinosaur bones,
🚇 K5 ☒ 260 Yan'an Donglu ☎ 6321 3548 ⏰ Daily 9–4:30 🚌 71 ♿ None 💷 Inexpensive

SHANGHAI ZOO
This is more enlightened than many Chinese zoos and provides an opportunity to see some of China's many rare or unique indigenous species. The zoo is located near the airport on land once owned by the Sassoon family (➤ 46).
🚇 Off map to west ☒ Hongqiao Lu (near airport) ⏰ Daily 9–4:30 🍴 Restaurants 🚌 57 ♿ None 💷 Inexpensive

TOY MARKET
This covered market in the Old Town seems to be entirely devoted to toys. The quality varies, but there is something for all ages. The play area is a plus.
🚇 K6 ☒ Fangbang Zhonglu near Danfeng Lu ⏰ Daily 🚌 11 ♿ None 💷 Inexpensive

XU BINJIE'S COLLECTION OF BOAT MODELS
This small museum, in the collector's own home, is one of several private collections in Shanghai. Enterprising collectors open their doors to the public for a small charge.
🚇 L4 ☒ No 131, Lane 1143, Dongyuhan Lu ⏰ Daily 🚌 25, 55 ♿ None 💷 Inexpensive

SHANGHAI
where to...

SHANGHAI-STYLE RESTAURANTS

Prices

Approximate prices for a meal for two excluding drinks:

$ = up to 100 yuan

$$ = 100–200 yuan

$$$ = more than 200 yuan

Most restaurants serve alcoholic drinks in the form of beer (Chinese and imported) and, increasingly, wine. Expensive imported brandies are often available as well as Chinese spirits such as *maotai* (which are an acquired taste but worth trying once).

Soup

Whereas in the West it is customary to have soup as an appetizer, in China soup is generally served towards the end of the meal as a sort of "*digestif*," and on informal occasions is also a way of helping to finish what is left in the rice bowl. At formal functions such as banquets, soup is served in a separate bowl.

1931 CAFÉ PUB ($–$$)

Although this is not just a restaurant, it does serve good Shanghai snacks (beef soup noodles, seafood congee) and dishes from other parts of China in a small area in a relaxed way. Old Shanghai prints line the walls.

➕ G6 ✉ 112 Maoming Nanlu ☎ 6472 5264 🕐 Dinner 🚍 24

BAI HUA YUAN ($$–$$$)

Refined cooking in the plush surroundings of the Sheraton Hotel, in the southwest corner of the city.

➕ C9 ✉ 1200 Caoxi Beilu ☎ 6439 6000 🕐 Lunch, dinner 🚇 Gymnasium 🚍 42, 43, 73

CITY RESTAURANT ($$–$$$)

Centrally located, close to the Nanking Road, in the old Metropole Hotel, this restaurant serves Cantonese as well as Shanghainese food. In its day, the Metropole was said to serve the best food in town—it is still excellent, as is the service.

➕ K5 ✉ 180 Jiangxi Zhonglu ☎ 6321 3030 🕐 Lunch, dinner 🚍 64

FORUM PALACE SEAFOOD ($$–$$$)

Cantonese snacks and Shanghai seafood (especially dim sum and savory snacks) in a plush, modern setting in the heart of the old French Concession. Alert service.

➕ J6 ✉ 188 Huaihai Zhonglu ☎ 6386 2608 🕐 Lunch, dinner 🚍 26

THE GRAPE ($$)

Close to an old Russian Orthodox church, the service is very friendly and the Shanghai and Yangzhou cooking, reliable. Try the Yangzhou fried rice, the salt-and-pepper pork chops and the claypot eggplant with vermicelli.

➕ G6 ✉ 55 Xinle Lu ☎ 6472 0486 🕐 Lunch, dinner 🚍 45

HAI YU LAN GE ($$–$$$)

Good local cooking in the Sofitel Hyland Hotel, just 15 minutes' walk from the Bund.

➕ K5 ✉ 505 Nanjing Donglu ☎ 6351 5888 🕐 Lunch, dinner 🚍 27

HUA DU ($$)

This centrally situated restaurant in the modernized Jing An Hotel, specializes in Shanghai seafood dishes including eels, crab, red-stewed fish and smoked carp.

➕ F5 ✉ 370 Huashan Lu ☎ 6248 1888 🕐 Breakfast, lunch, dinner 🚍 45, 48

LAO FANDIAN ($$–$$$)

Something of an institution in the Old Town, this modernized version of an old restaurant (whose name means old restaurant) serves Shanghai dishes, including noodles, and seafood according to the season.

➕ K6 ✉ 242 Fuyou Lu, Old Town ☎ 6328 2782 🕐 Lunch, dinner 🚍 11

LULU'S ($–$$)

A good place late at night when you want simple but authentic Shanghainese food. Try the drunken shrimp, minced soya and vegetables and fermented rice soup.

🚩 G5 ✉ 69 Shimen 1-Lu ☎ 6258 5645 🍽 Lunch, dinner 🚌 41

MEI LONG ZHEN ($$)

This restaurant is in an early 20th-century building that was once the the Communist Party headquarters. The food served here is in the Huaiyang and Sichuan styles, as well as Shanghainese. Deep-fried *gui* (fish), beans in hot peanut sauce, spicy fried octopus, various tofu dishes and cold shredded jellyfish are interesting and worth trying.

🚩 G5 ✉ 1081 Nanjing Xilu ☎ 6253 5353 🍽 Lunch, dinner 🚌 37

MERRY LIN ($$–$$$)

Modern and comfortable furnishings are the background to usually excellent and authentic Shanghai cooking with good service. A little out of the way but not far from the American Consulate. Garlic spinach and beef with oyster sauce and onions are highly recommended.

🚩 E6 ✉ 1 Wulumuqi Nanlu ☎ 6466 6363 🍽 Lunch, dinner 🚌 93

MOON SHANGHAI ($$)

A restaurant that is patronized by locals and visitors alike, in a residential area, just off Huaihai Zhonglu. The dishes are not elaborate, but they are well prepared. Examples are cold tofu and preserved egg and deep-fried *gui* (fish).

🚩 H6 ✉ Lane 28, 833 Huaihai Zhonglu ☎ 6471 7330 🍽 Lunch and dinner 🚌 26

SHANGHAI EXPRESS ($$–$$$)

Solid Shanghai cooking in a pleasant restaurant in the Shanghai Hilton where the standard of service is high. Open 24 hours a day.

🚩 F5 ✉ 250 Huashan Lu ☎ 6248 0000 🍽 Breakfast, lunch, dinner 🚌 45

SHANGHAI RESTAURANT ($$–$$$)

A wide range of local specialties (► 61) including Dazha crab and stir-fried eels are served in the bright, modern surroundings of the Jianguo Hotel.

🚩 D8 ✉ 439 Caoxi Beilu ☎ 6439 9299 🍽 Lunch, dinner 🚌 42, 43, 50

THE VILLAGE RESTAURANT ($–$$)

The food in this two-storey restaurant is Cantonese as well as Shanghainese. It's popular among expatriates and locals for its quality and reasonable prices. The chicken and bamboo soup is excellent.

🚩 D7 ✉ 137 Tianping Lu ☎ 6282 8018 🍽 Lunch, dinner 🚌 26

Soy sauce

Soy sauce is an important seasoning agent in Chinese cooking, providing flavor and saltiness. Many Westerners like to add the sauce to their rice, something that adult Chinese regard with amusement, since normally only children do this.

OTHER CHINESE REGIONAL CUISINES

Tea

Tea is the main accompaniment to meals for most Chinese. Cold water is thought to be unhealthy for the stomach—indeed it is not uncommon for people to drink hot water with their meals. Tea in Shanghai is normally green, that is to say, made with unfermented leaves.

A WENG THAI SHARKFIN ($$)

This bright, modern restaurant specializes in a mix of Thai and Chinese cooking and is noted for its Thai puddings which are sold during the afternoon. Recommended dishes are steamed asparagus, Thai chicken salad and the hot and sour vermicelli .

✚ F5 ✉ 38 Yanan Xi Lu
☎ 6248 7924 ◷ Lunch, dinner
🚌 26

CHUNG KONG DREAM GARDEN ($$–$$$)

Specializing in the Cantonese and Chaozhou fare, this restaurant close to the Jin Jiang Hotel in the old French Concession serves Taiwan prawns and steamed sharkfin.

✚ G6 ✉ 59 Maoming Nanlu
☎ 6258 2582 ◷ Lunch, dinner
🚌 126, 42

DYNASTY ($$$)

The sort of plush Chinese restaurant usually found in Hong Kong and Singapore, this hotel dining room offers creative Cantonese-style cooking, including lobster *sashimi* and pork in lotus leaf. It's a long way from the center, however.

✚ A5 ✉ Yang Zi Jiang Hotel, 2099 Yan'an Xilu ☎ 6275 0000
◷ Lunch, dinner 🚌 57

FENGHE ($–$$)

There's a relaxed atmosphere here, with modern furnishings and gentle live music in the evenings. The menu offers reasonably priced dishes from all over China. Sample the crab and noodles claypot and *yangcen* (fried rice).

✚ K6 ✉ 96 Sichuan Nanlu

☎ 6328 3992 ◷ Lunch, dinner
🚇 126

FU LIN XUAN ($$–$$$)

Cantonese seafood. The glass and wood décor is stylish and the food pretty good, though service is variable.

✚ H6 ✉ 37 Sinan Lu
☎ 6372 1777 ◷ Lunch, dinner
🚌 24

THE GAP ($$–$$$)

There are two versions of this quirky restaurant (the second is at 8 Zunyi Lu). The more central of the two is close to the Jin Jiang Hotel and features an old car clinging precariously above the entrance. The atmosphere inside is southern European with wood paneling and plants. The food is mixed in style, with an emphasis on north Chinese cooking.

✚ G6 ✉ 127 Maoming Nanlu
☎ 6433 9028 ◷ Lunch, dinner
🚌 126

HANSE ($$)

Spread over three stories with Latin American-style decor, this restaurant serves Fuzhou style food. Mixed seafood and seafood dumplings are typical dishes.

✚ B4 ✉ 121 Zunyi Lu
☎ 6259 8388 ◷ Lunch, dinner
🚌 69

HARBOR SEAFOOD ($$)

The Chaozhou-style fare here includes dishes such as goose liver and steamed *huatiao* (crab). Thai and Japanese dishes available.

✚ G6 ✉ 4th Floor, 778 Huaihai Zhonglu ☎ 6433 7286
◷ Lunch, dinner 🚌 26

HUAI SIAN LOU ($$–$$$)

A glitzy restaurant in one of the new department stores. The Cantonese food is fairly expensive but extremely well prepared—the suckling pig and crispy chicken noodles are excellent.

H6 ✉ 7th floor of Isetan Department Store, 527 Huaihai Zhonglu ☎ 5306 1616 ⏱ Lunch, dinner 🚌 26

JIA JIA LE ($)

Specializing in the Malaysian and Singaporean versions of Chinese food, this is a good place to get snacks—Hainan chicken, tofu in a peanut sauce, sago pudding and jasmine rice. It is also open for breakfast.

F8 ✉ 1351 Xietu Lu ☎ 6404 9050 ⏱ Breakfast, lunch, dinner 🚌 89

LAO CHENGDU SICHUAN ($$–$$$)

Bright and modern restaurant on two floors. Serves Sichuan music and food to include smoked duck, tofu with hot minced beef and cold sesame sauce noodles.

B5 ✉ 1733 Yanan Xilu ☎ 6219 4583 ⏱ Lunch, dinner 🚌 57

LE JARDIN ($–$$)

Located in a hotel, where you can relax to the sound of a bubbling fountain, this is a coffee shop that has a large menu specializing in dishes from southeast Asia which include West Lake congee, udon noodle soup, *nasi goreng* and shredded pork. European dishes are also available.

Off map (D10) ✉ Novotel Yuanlin Hotel, 201 Baise Lu

☎ 6470 1688 ⏱ Breakfast, lunch, dinner

LILAC GARDEN ($$–$$$)

Close to one of the oldest European buildings in Shanghai, this relaxed restaurant specializes in subtle, well-presented Cantonese and Sichuan cooking,

E6 ✉ 849 Huashan Lu ☎ 6252 5400 ⏱ Lunch, dinner 🚌 48, 113

MEI GIAO ($$$)

A sophisticated restaurant serving a variety of Chinese dishes which have been given the gourmet touch through the delicate use of spices.

G5 ✉ 120 Jinxian Lu ☎ 6256 4168 ⏱ Lunch, dinner 🚌 42, 104

PAN ASIAN RESTAURANT ($$–$$$)

Modern resaurant with traditional Thai features in the Shanghai Hotel. Specializes in tropical style Chinese and southeast Asian dishes, including Hainan chicken rice, Singapore vermicelli, crab fried rice, chicken curry and yam soup .

E5 ✉ Shanghai Hotel, Wulumuqi Lu ☎ 6249 0998 ext. 6234 ⏱ Lunch, dinner 🚌 48

SICHUAN RESTAURANT ($–$$)

This restaurant has been around for a long time, and the food—spicy Sichuanese but not impossibly hot—is still delicious. And the prices are not bad.

H5 ✉ 457 Nanjing Donglu ☎ 6322 2247 ⏱ Lunch, dinner 🚌 20, 37

Dessert

For most Westerners, even those who adore Chinese food, the one thing missing from a meal is something truly sweet at the end. Desserts are not a big feature of Chinese meals, but banana cooked in a toffee sauce, and Eight Treasure Rice—a delicious, if slightly heavy concoction of rice, honey and fruit—are especially good.

OTHER CHINESE REGIONAL CUISINES

SUNYA ($–$$$)

Reliable Cantonese restaurant with two floors—the lower one is more informal while the upper floor is more expensive. Food is good on both floors.

🚇 J5 ✉ Rebuilt ☎ 6351 7788 🕐 Lunch, dinner 🚌 27

XIAO SHAOXING ($$–$$$)

Spread over three floors (with the top one being more formal), this restaurant serves mixed Chinese food and specializes in "white cut chicken" (cold marinated chicken).

🚇 H5 ✉ 473 Nanjing Xilu ☎ 6327 8254 🕐 Lunch, dinner 🚌 20, 27

Also at: 🚇 J5 ✉ 75 Yunnan Lu ☎ 6373 2890 🕐 Lunch, dinner 🚌 20, 27

VEGETARIAN

GONGDELIN ($–$$)

A well-known and popular restaurant with a branch in Beijing. This long-established restaurant, with a central location, serves vegetarian dishes presented as imitations (using tofu) of meat dishes—for example mock chicken and mock duck.

🚇 J5 ✉ 445 Nanjing Xilu ☎ 6327 0218 🕐 Lunch, dinner 🚌 20, 27

HARN SHEH ($)

Specializes in Taiwanese snacks and fruit teas, including cold papaya tea and *taro ball* milk tea.

🚇 D7 ✉ 10 Hengshan Lu ☎ 6474 6547 🕐 Lunch, dinner 🚇 Xujiahui

JADE BUDDHA TEMPLE ($)

Reasonably priced vegetarian restaurant serving well-prepared regional dishes in the city's most famous temple.

🚇 G3 ✉ 170 Anyuan Lu ☎ 6266 3668 🕐 Lunch 🚌 105, 106

JUELIN VEGETARIAN RESTAURANT ($–$$)

A good selection of vegetarian dishes is delightfully presented in this restaurant in a central location, near the Bund. There is an added attraction of a Buddhist shrine on the ground floor.

🚇 K6 ✉ 250 Jinling Lu ☎ 6326 0115 🕐 Lunch, early dinner 🚌 42

TIAN TIAN WANG ($–$$)

This restaurant serves vegetarian dishes made with tea—red tea quail eggs, tea powder vegetables, and tealeaf ginseng shreds. Also worth trying are the fried radish cake and steamed egg-white skin dumplings.

🚇 D5 ✉ 48 Lane 1088, Yuyuan lu ☎ 6212 5758 🕐 Lunch, dinner 🚌 20, 21

VILLAGE RESTAURANT ($$)

Although not specifically a vegetarian restaurant there are a number of dishes which should appeal to vegetarians, including parsley soup, crispy-skin tofu, and minced greens with tofu. Welcoming atmosphere and attentive.

🚇 D7 ✉ 137 Tianping Lu ☎ 6282 8018 🕐 Lunch, dinner 🚌 26

WESTERN RESTAURANTS

THE ATRIUM CAFÉ ($$–$$$)

A high ceilinged, modern restaurant serving a wide range of foods from different countries, from Chinese through to Continental European and Middle Eastern dishes. Excellent breakfast buffets, Sunday brunch, seafood, Lebanese food and Viennese pastries.

⊞ K5 ✉ 236 Zhongshan Dong 1-Lu (Bund) ☎ 6323 9379 ⊙ Lunch, dinner 🚌 22, 126, 42, 55

BLUE MOUNTAIN CAFÉ ($$)

Modern café that serves reasonably priced Continental European food, including club sandwiches and salads as well as coffee.

⊞ E7 ✉ Hengshan Hotel, 526 Hengshan Lu ☎ 6437 7050 ext.637 ⊙ Breakfast, lunch, dinner 🚌 15, 42, 49

THE BUND ($$–$$$)

Steak Diane, cherries jubilee and other French dishes are served amid sophisticated, plush European-style surroundings in the Jin Jiang Tower hotel.

⊞ G6 ✉ 161 Changle Lu ☎ 6415 1188 ext.80411 ⊙ Breakfast, lunch, dinner 🚌 41

THE CAFÉ ($$–$$$)

A spacious rustic-style hotel café which is open 24 hours a day. There is a buffet of European dishes each day, a patisserie and made-to-order dishes such as omelettes, pasta and burgers.

⊞ F5 ✉ Equatorial Hotel, 65 Yan'an Xilu ☎ 6248 1688 ⊙ Breakfast, lunch, dinner 🚌 71

CAFÉ DE LA SEINE ($–$$)

Essentially a bar, but one which also serves snacks such as filled baguettes, cakes, croissants and a few other French-influenced dishes. Excellent location by the Huangpu River.

⊞ K5 ✉ 236 Zhongshan Dong 1-Lu (Bund) ☎ 6323 9379 ⊙ Lunch, dinner 🚌 22, 126, 42, 55

CAPPUCCINO ($$)

Within the Equatorial Hotel and with an Italian café décor, this restaurant is devoted mainly to pasta dishes, including *fettuccini alla pescatora* and *rigatoni all'arrabbiata*, and pizzas as well as sublime tiramisu.

⊞ F5 ✉ 65 Yan'an Xilu ☎ 6248 1688 ext.2384 ⊙ Lunch, dinner 🚌 48, 71

CHURCHILL'S PUB AND DELI ($–$$)

You'll find the atmosphere of a traditional English pub, and the British chef prepares snacks, afternoon teas and pub grub, including ploughman's lunch, Irish stew and English puddings such as treacle pudding.

⊞ F6 ✉ Dong Hu Hotel, 167 Xinle Lu ☎ 6415 8158 ext.12131 ⊙ Lunch, dinner 🚌 45

EURO'S RESTAURANT ($$)

Specializing in European food in general and

Chez Louis

Until about 1993, Western food was not really a sensible option and the only place professing to serve a Western meal was a peculiar survivor of pre-war Shanghai, the former Chez Louis, which survived as The Red House. Here you could eat idiosyncratic versions of tournedos Rossini and Grand Marnier soufflé. In its latest incarnation, the Red House can be found on Huaihai Lu (✉ 845 Huaihai Zhonglu ☎ 6437 4902).

Expensive options

Always check the cost of dishes which do not have a price on the menu. Seasonal dishes, particularly those involving seafoods can be very expensive, even on an otherwise inexpensive menu.

German in particular, the German chef produces such delicacies as Nuremberger sausages, pork knuckles, goulash and banana fritters.

➕ C9 ✉ Olympic Hotel, 1800 Zhongshan Nan 2-Lu ☎ 6439 6010 ⏰ Lunch, dinner ▣ 73

FEST BREW HOUSE ($–$$)

A beerhall that sells the only home-brewed beer in Shanghai, as well as the dishes to go with it— baked fish, oxtail soup, pork Lyonnaise.

➕ K5 ✉ 11 Hankou Lu ☎ 6323 0965 ⏰ Lunch, dinner ▣ 49

FIFTY HANKOU LU ($$)

In a spacious pre-war building which used to be a bank, that's now decorated in Indonesian style and in an excellent location near the Bund, this restaurant serves an eclectic mix of European and Asian dishes as well as afternoon tea. The *laksa lemak*, lamb korma and Makhani chicken are the specialties here.

➕ K5 ✉ 50 Hankou Lu ☎ 6323 8383 ⏰ Lunch, dinner ▣ 49

GOLDEN WORLD ($$)

The gaudy, burlesque decoration here lends a cinematic feel to this popular restaurant, which often features a pianist and singers in the evenings. Serves dishes such as various pastas, salads, smoked salmon and a range of cakes. The menu changes daily and it is worth telephoning

ahead for details of the dishes of the day.

➕ F5 ✉ 139 Yan'an Xilu ☎ 6248 5510 ⏰ Lunch, dinner ▣ 71

JUDY'S TWO ($$)

Modern, comfortable and spacious bar and restaurant on two floors that's at once Western and Chinese. There is also a small terrace for alfresco eating. Dishes include pastas, sirloin steaks, soups, and salads.

➕ G6 ✉ 176 Maoming Nanlu ☎ 6473 1417 ⏰ Lunch, dinner ▣ 96

LONG BAR ($$)

Decorated to give the flavor of pre-war Shanghai, this is essentially a bar (with juke box) which also serves substantial Western and Chinese snacks.

➕ G5 ✉ Shanghai Center, 1376 Nanjing Xilu ☎ 6279 8268 ⏰ Lunch, dinner ▣ 20, 37

TICINO ($$–$$$)

A European chef produces the Italo-Swiss food such as rabbit stew and polenta, squid remoulade, *bresaola* as well as apple-and-raisin polenta cake. Ultra-modern monochrome interior.

➕ N7 ✉ New Asia Tomson Hotel, 777 Zhangyang Lu ☎ 5831 8888 ⏰ Lunch, dinner ▣ 119

SNACKS & STREET FOOD

In a country where the cooking is of such high quality and where food in general is so important (it is even considered medicinal), it is a curious thing that Western fast-food has become so popular. Hamburgers and fried chicken have arrived and are available on every main street but it is really worth avoiding all that in favor of true Chinese fast food (dumplings and noodles, for example). They're cheaper, healthier and a great deal more delicious. Where Western snacks win is in the ice-cream and the cake department.

AMERICAN 33 ICE CREAM ($)

Ice cream plus simple Chinese dishes such as broiled chicken and noodles.

➕ G5 ✉ 1012 Nanjing Xilu ☎ 6217 8051 🕐 Breakfast, lunch, dinner 🚌 20, 27

AROMA CAKESHOP ($)

A counter in the Asia Tomson Hotel in Pudong sells a wide selection of good cakes, breads, and pastries.

➕ Off map to east ✉ 1st Floor, Asia Tomson Hotel, 777 Zhangyang Lu, Pudong 🕐 All day ☎ 5831 8888 🚌 119

CHAMPS ELYSÉES ($)

Small open-air café in front of the Printemps Department Store—ice creams, tea, coffee, and other drinks.

➕ H6 ✉ Huaihai Zhonglu at the intersection with Shanxi Lu 🕐 Lunch, dinner 🚌 911 ,42

HAAGEN-DAZS ICE CREAM PARLOR ($)

The international chain of premium ice-cream cafés has now reached Shanghai in this café, near the Nanking Road and the Bund, with seating for almost a hundred customers. There is also a take-out service.

➕ K5 ✉ 401 Henan Zhonglu ☎ 6352 6184 🕐 Lunch, dinner 🚌 37

KOTOBUKI BAKERY ($)

Part of a Japanese chain, the Kotobuki sells a variety of Western-style cakes, breads, and light snacks.

➕ G6 ✉ 919 Huaihai Zhonglu ☎ 6253 0534 🕐 Shopping hours
Also at
➕ D7 ✉ Orient Shopping Center , Xujiahui
and at ➕ J3 ✉ 218 Tianmu Lu

PUCCI ($)

Good fresh pastries, doughnuts, cookies, and dairy products in the Isetan Department Store.

➕ H6 ✉ 1st Floor, Isetan, Huaihai Zhonglu ☎ 6375 1111 🕐 Shopping hours 🚌 26

SOFITEL DELI ($/$$)

This attractive delicatessen, located in the reception area of the Sofitel Hyland Hotel, sells cakes, cookies, and pastries. About a 15-minute walk from the Bund.

➕ K5 ✉ Sofitel Hyland Hotel, 505 Nanjing Donglu 🕐 All day 🚌 37

Hygiene

The standard of hygiene in China is generally reliable. Food preparers buy fresh ingredients and ensure that ingredients are thoroughly cooked. Street food is normally safe although it is wise to avoid meat and choose vegetable dishes from street vendors.

Local snacks

One of the specialties of the region is Ningbo or "pigeon egg" dumplings, little balls of sticky rice enclosing a delicious sweet osmanthus paste. Another snack is "zhong zhi," sticky rice with meat wrapped in a lotus leaf. To find these and other delicious snacks, stop in the Old Town—both in the area of the Huxingting Tea House and on the streets around it, where there are a large number of small restaurants (S) and stalls.

➕ H6 🚌 26

ANTIQUES, CRAFTS & SOUVENIRS

ANTIQUES

There are also a number of markets specializing in antiques and bric-à-brac (➤ 56–7).

FRIENDSHIP STORE

Large selection of interesting, though expensive, antiques including good quality porcelain and cloisonné.

➕ L5 ✉ 40 Beijing Donglu ☎ 6329 7374 🕐 Daily 9AM–10PM

FRIENDSHIP STORE, ANTIQUES BRANCH

A specialist branch of the Friendship Store with an extensive range of all types of genuine Chinese antiques. Also stocks some good pieces of cloisonné.

➕ J5 ✉ 694 Nanjing Xilu ☎ 6253 8092 🚌 37

LANQIN JEWELLERY & CULTURE RELIC FIRM

Jewelry, antiques and general souvenirs. Not the highest quality, but the sort of place where you might find the occasional bargain.

➕ G6 ✉ 398 Changle Lu ☎ 6255 1667 🚌 41

NANQUAN COLLECTION STORE

Mostly handicrafts but also a small selection of antiques and curiosities.

➕ J9 ✉ 159 Jiangbian Lu ☎ 6377 0101 🚌 45, 66

SHANGHAI ANTIQUE & CURIO STORE

Reliable and established store found close to the Bund, selling porcelain, jewelry, silk embroidery, paintings and many other antique items.

➕ K5 ✉ 192–240 Guangdong Lu ☎ 6321 4697 🕐 Daily 9–5 🚌 66

SHANGHAI G-E-TANG ANTIQUE CO. LTD.

High-quality antique Chinese furniture. Centrally located as part of an antiques market. Shipping can be arranged all over the world.

➕ J6 ✉ 2/F, 50 Liuhekou Lu ☎ 6384 6388 🚌 17, 18, 23

SHANGHAI G-E-TANG ANTIQUE CO. LTD.

Large warehouse near the airport belonging to the company described above.

➕ Off map to west ✉ 399 Lao Hu Qing Ping Gong Lu 🚌 Warehouse, no telephone number

HANDICRAFTS & SOUVENIRS

CHINA TOURIST SOUVENIR CORPORATION

Huge store selling handicraft items, antique imitations, and souvenirs from around the country. The advantage here is the large range of merchandise under one roof.

➕ G5 ✉ Shanghai Exhibition Center, 1000 Yan'an Zhonglu ☎ 6279 0279 🚌 49, 71

FRIENDSHIP STORE

(➤ Antiques, above)

SHANGHAI ARTS & CRAFTS IMPORT AND EXPORT CORPORATION SALES DEPARTMENT

Jewelry, ornaments, traditional wooden furniture, embroidery,

Antiques

It is illegal to export anything older than 150 years. A red seal on an antique will tell you that it is genuine and exportable. There are so many stores and market stall holders selling antiques that the seal of approval may be absent. There is no sure-fire method of knowing what you are buying (except when the seal is present) other than to ignore what you are told by the seller and really inspect the object in question. Some of the imitations are of a very high standad but are often marked, on the bottom, as being authentic reproductions. This is information that salesmen are unlikely to volunteer of course, but if you like the item it will still be cheaper than the real thing! Note that shipping is available in only a few stores.

paintings, calligraphy materials and general handicrafts.

📍 L4 ✉ 817 Daming Lu ☎ 6546 3066 🚌 28

SHANGHAI ARTS & CRAFTS SERVICE CENTER

Jadeware, embroideries, ivory carving, leather goods, carpets, gold, and silver in an accessible location adjacent to the Park Hotel and opposite the old racetrack.

📍 J5 ✉ 190 Nanjing Xilu ☎ 6327 5299 🚌 20, 37

SHANGHAI FOREIGN TRADE EMPORIUM

Handicraft items and also general shopping including clothes and medicines.

📍 K5 ✉ 24 Nanjing Donglu ☎ 6323 0148 🚌 37

SHANGHAI GOODWILL STORE

General handicrafts, souvenirs and patent medicines

📍 F4 ✉ 1700 Beijing Xilu ☎ 6258 4213 🚌 15, 21

YI HUA LACE & EMBROIDERY STORE

Specializes in table linen and garments in traditional Chinese style.

📍 D6 ✉ 1932 Huashan Lu ☎ 6438 7378 🚌 48

PORCELAIN

GUO HUA CHINAWARE STORE

It is mainly the modern, gaudy style of Chinese porcelain that is on sale here.

📍 J5 ✉ 550 Nanjing Donglu 🚌 27

SHANGHAI JINGDEZHEN PORCELAIN ARTWARE SERVICE DEPT.

Porcelain and handicraft articles.

📍 F5 ✉ 1175 Nanjing Xilu ☎ 6253 0885 🚌 20, 37

JEWELRY & ENAMEL

Bronze ornaments are covered in a network of copper strips and then filled with layers of enamel paint, before being fired and polished—this is cloisonné. Good pieces are hard to find, the best tend to be found among the antiques.

JUKAI ENTERPRISE LTD.

Jewels, gold and silver work and handicrafts.

📍 G5 ✉ 1376 Nanjing Xilu ☎ 6279 8335 🚌 20, 37

SHANGHAI LYCEUM JEWELRY & ANTIQUE STORE

Antiques, jewelry, paintings, porcelain, seals.

📍 G6 ✉ 398 Changle Lu ☎ 6255 1667 🚌 41, 96

SHENG LI ENAMEL STORE

Specializes in a wide variety of items of enamelware with exquisite examples of cloisonné .

📍 J5 ✉ 214 Yan'an Donglu ☎ 6321 7628 🚌 42

Silk

One of the bargains in China is silk, which even today should be cheaper than at home. It may be difficult to find silk in pure colors, or with modern designs—the Chinese prefer patterned silk with designs that can be considered old-fashioned. Bear in mind that many items of silk clothing that seem such good value wil never be the same after cleaning, even dry cleaning.

THIS & THAT

The Four Treasures of the Study

Traditionally, scholars took great pride in the art of calligraphy, setting great store by the quality of their brushes, paper and inksticks and ink stones (ornamental slabs with a shallow receptacle for water into which the inkstick is dipped to create the paint). These are known collectively as the "Four Treasures of the Study."

TEA ARTICLES

Although the most immediately attractive gifts and souvenirs are to be found in the large emporiums and stores aimed at visitors, some of the most worthwhile purchases are to be found in the smaller stores that specialize in items connected with daily life. Among China's real bargains are teapots, the most famous of which are made in Shanghai's neighboring province of Jiangsu. Known as Yixing ware, they are in fact made in Dingshu. It is said that the quality of the ceramic is so high that excellent tea can be made just by adding water to an old Yixing pot.

HUANGSHAN TEA CO.

Everything required for tea including Yixing teapots and other delightful ceramics.
✚ G6 ✉ 853 Huaihai Zhonglu
☎ 6373 9759 🚌 42, 911

WRITING AND PAINTING MATERIALS AND BOOKS

The idea of buying a Chinese book may seem rather pointless if you are unable to read Chinese. However, there are many Chinese books published in English and other foreign languages. Among them are books of classic poetry and prose, illustrated books (for example, on the architecture of Shanghai or on classic Chinese art)

and illustrated children's stories. Another good buy are calendars (which are often for sale in bookstores) some of which are beautifully decorated with prints of classic Chinese paintings. Artists find that Chinese brushes are a good buy, while inkstones and inksticks, even if never used, are very attractive ornaments.

CHINESE ANCIENT BOOKSTORE

Antiquarian books, paintings, stationery and items required for calligraphy.
✚ K5 ✉ 424 Fuzhou Lu
☎ 6322 3453 🚌 17, 49

DUO YUN XUAN ART STUDIO

Calligraphy and paintings, stationery, rubbings of ancient carvings, and seals.
✚ K5 ✉ 422 Nanjing Donglu
☎ 6350 4882 🚌 37

LAO ZHOU HU CHENG CHINESE WRITING BRUSH AND INKSTICK STORE

As the name suggests, this store specializes in the items needed for traditional Chinese painting and calligraphy—brushes, inkstones and ink slabs, for example.
✚ K5 ✉ 90 Henan Zhonglu
☎ 6323 0924 🚌 66

JIN JIANG HOTEL BOOKSTORE

Within the precincts of the old Jin Jiang Hotel is this store selling all types of books about most aspects of Shanghai and China.

➕ G6 ✉ 59 Maoming Nanlu
☎ 6472 1273 🚌 126

SHANGHAI FOREIGN LANGUAGES BOOKSTORE

Sells all types of books in foreign languages, including in English, including books on Shanghai, as well as CDs and stationery.
➕ K5 ✉ 390 Fuzhou Lu
☎ 6322 3200 🚌 17, 49

SHANGHAI MUSEUM STORE

In fact, there are three stores on the southern side of the museum that specialize in books (in Chinese and foreign languages), antiques and antique reproductions.
➕ J5 ✉ 201 Renmin Dadao
☎ 6372 8522 🚌 23

STAMPS

SHANGHAI PHILATELIC CORPORATION

Sells new editions of Chinese stamps and a few used ones.
➕ K5 ✉ 244 Nanjing Donglu
🚌 27

PHOTOGRAPHY

The main problem for avid photographers is to find supplies of slide film, and even more difficult to locate are supplies of black-and-white film. If you want to use these, then bring as much as you think you will need, and more.

KEYI PHOTOGRAPHY

Centrally located photography store, selling Chinese and imported film and equipment.
➕ K5 ✉ 150 Nanjing Donglu
☎ 6323 1212 🚌 37

WAN KAI PHOTO CO.

Sells photographic equipment from a easily accessed location on the Nanking Road.
➕ J5 ✉ 673 Nanjing Donglu
☎ 6322 1098 🚌 20, 37

CLOTHES

Probably the best place for clothes shopping is the Huaihai Road, the main street of the former French Concession, where there are several stores specializing in designer clothes imported from Hong Kong and other designer labels have appeared in the last few years.

CROCODILE INTERNATIONAL

Imported Hong Kong and international designer clothes sold in a bright modern store.
➕ G6 ✉ 328–32 Shanxi Nanlu ☎ 6327 7459 🚌 104

ESPRIT

International style off-the-peg clothes. Now has its own franchise in some big department stores like Isetan.
➕ H6 ✉ 224–30 Huaihai Zhonglu ☎ 3281 531 🚌 26

PIERRE CARDIN

Shanghai branch of the expensive French designer specializing in leather goods and handbags. As you would expect, the décor is modern.
➕ F5 ✉ 338 Huashan Lu
☎ 6248 3272 🚌 48

Older stores

All the new department stores are the equal of anything in the world, but some of the more traditional stores are still worth a look. Drop into the stationery and bookstores along Fuzhou Lu, for example, where there are bargains like beautiful calendars for sale.

DEPARTMENT STORES, SUPERMARKETS & TRADITIONAL MEDICINES

DEPARTMENT STORES

HUA LIAN

This is the former No. 10 Department Store which, before the war, was the renowned Wing On Department Store, in its day the latest thing in shopping. It has now been reborn as an international-style shopping center.

➕ J5 ✉ 635 Nanjing Donglu
☎ 6322 4466 🚌 20, 37

ISETAN

Tokyo-based department store selling all the world's latest wares, though concentrating on items from Japan.

➕ H6 ✉ 537 Huaihai Zhonglu
☎ 5306 1111 🚌 911, 42

KINTETSU DEPARTMENT STORE

A wide range of daily necessities—clothing, foods, electronic goods—is available here at reasonable prices.

➕ G5 ✉ 1376 Nanjing Xilu
☎ 6278 9376

NEW WORLD DEPARTMENT STORE

Housed partly in one of the old pre-war entertainment centers, this was a precursor to the recently resurrected Great World Center (➤ 40), and linked to its other half by means of a walkway across the street. This has been transformed into a full-scale department store selling all kinds of goods, including cosmetics, traditional medicines and foodstuffs, electronic goods and clothes.

➕ J5 ✉ 2 Nanjing Xilu
☎ 6358 8888 🚌 20, 37

SHANGHAI NO. 1 DEPARTMENT STORE

Located in one of the old pre-war department store buildings, this old stalwart has been modernized and offers a wide range of Chinese and international goods.

➕ J5 ✉ 830 Nanjing Donglu
☎ 6322 3344 🚌 20, 37

SUPERMARKETS & FOOD STORES

In the same way that the old department stores have been transformed, so it is with food stores and supermarkets. Until comparatively recently, there was no real prospect of being able to buy foods that would have appealed to Westerners except in the Friendship Stores. Most Chinese stores sold only poor quality fruit, uninteresting sweets and candies and packaged and canned foods that were not very palatable to the uninitiated. Now, not only are the local stores selling Chinese items that are hygenically and attractively packaged, but there are supermarkets in the department stores and chains of smaller mini-supermarkets which all sell goods from around the world .

CARREFOUR

Good French-based international grocery store selling Western groceries and household items at reasonable prices.

➕ M1 ✉ 560 Quyang Lu, Hongkou ☎ 6555 8078

FRIENDSHIP GROCERY STORE

This store, just behind the main building of the Friendship Store, sells Western and Chinese groceries.

➕ K5 ✉ 40 Beijing Donglu ☎ 6323 1419 🚌 37

HAM & PICKLES STORE, BEI WAN YOU QUAN

Store specializing in cured meats and vegetables, but also a wide range of Chinese foodstuffs.

➕ K5 ✉ 285 Nanjing Donglu ☎ 6322 1474 🚌 37

JIN JANG GROCERY STORE

All sorts of Western and Chinese groceries with bakery counter, stationery and toiletries.

➕ G6 ✉ 175 Changle Lu ☎ 6258 2582 ext.9603 🚌 126

PARKSON GROCERY

A Western-style supermarket taking up one floor of the department store of the same name.

➕ H6 ✉ Parkson Department Store, 918 Huaihai Zhonglu ☎ 6415 8818 🚌 126, 911, 42

QUAN GUO NATIVE PRODUCTS & SPECIALTIES FOOD STORE

Various foods, including regional specialties from all over China.

➕ J6 ✉ 491 Huaihai Zhonglu ☎ 6372 1466 🚌 911, 42

SHANGHAI NO. 1 FOODSTORE

Sugars, teas, farm produce, cigarettes, wines, cooked meats.

➕ J5 ✉ 720 Nanjing Donglu ☎ 6322 2777 🚌 37

WELLCOME GROCERY STORE

Expensive but comprehensive Hong Kong supermarket selling Western and Japanese produce.

➕ G5 ✉ 1376 Nanjing Xilu ☎ 6279 8018 🚌 37

TRADITIONAL MEDICINES

A visit to a traditional Chinese pharmacy is always a worthwhile experience, if only to see all the exotic items for sale. The Chinese are very health conscious—even food is thought of as a form of medicine. There are some startling items on display—wines with snakes coiled up inside the bottle, for example.

CAI TONG DE DRUGSTORE

Specializes in traditional Chinese herbs and cures.

➕ J5 ✉ 320 Nanjing Donglu ☎ 6350 4740 🚌 37

TONG HAN CHUN TANG TRADITIONAL CHINESE MEDICINE STORE

Chinese herbal and traditional patent medicines and Western medical instruments.

➕ E5 ✉ 20 Yuyuan Lu ☎ 6373 1232 🚌 20, 21

BARS, PUBS & NIGHTLIFE

Hustlers

Whether Shanghai will ever be quite the venal place of the early 20th century is a moot point, but it is already trying to make up for lost time. The hustlers and the pimps are back and you should not be too surprised if you are propositioned on the street. Resist, or it may turn out to be an expensive experience.

Foreign influence

A lot of the pubs and bars are run by foreign residents, a commitment which reflects the confidence that most people now have in the future of Shanghai and of China. The big difference is that these establishments are not aimed exclusively at the expatriates but just as much at the newly-moneyed Chinese.

ALI BABA PUB
Of the two floors here, the lower is a sort of cocktail lounge and bar with gaudy murals while the upper floor, decorated with cosy printed wallpaper, has pool tables and comfortable chairs and dining areas.
✚ F5 ✉ 189 Yan'an Xilu ☎ 6249 5322 🕐 11PM–3AM 🚌 48

BLUES & JAZZ
The theme of the music played here is pre-war Shanghai and the music is in line with the name of the bar. Good German beer available.
✚ H6 ✉ 44 Sinan Lu ☎ 63272474 🕐 8PM–2AM 🚌 24

CAMERA L. A.
Pleasant place for a quiet drink and a snack with two rooms, one a bar, the other a café. The décor throughout is stucco and art prints.
✚ D6 ✉ 359 Xinhua Lu ☎ 6280 1256 🕐 2PM–2AM 🚌 48

CASABLANCA
This disco at the top of the Rainbow Hotel, west of the central area, is full of locals looking for a good time. Sleazy but entertaining and good fun if you firmly spurn unwanted overtures.
✚ B5 ✉ Rainbow Hotel, 2000 Yan'an Xilu ☎ 6275 3388 🕐 8:30PM–3AM 🚌 57

CHARLIE'S
One of the best hotel bars in the country (no longer quite the meaningless title it would have been a few years ago), this intimate, dark and lively bar is popular, professional yet friendly.
✚ D6 ✉ Holiday Inn Crowne Plaza, 400 Fanyu Lu ☎ 6252 8888 🕐 2PM–2AM 🚌 76

CLUB ABSOLUTE
Well known for its up-to-the-minute dance music, this is one of the most fashionable places in Shanghai.
✚ G6 ✉ 122 Shanxi Nanlu ☎ 6279 4999 🕐 9:30PM–2:30AM 🚌 42

COTTON CLUB
Nice little American-style bar—videos and pictures of American movie stars lend atmosphere—that has live rock music most evenings and serves snacks.
✚ F6 ✉ 8 Fuxing Xilu ☎ 6437 7110 🕐 8PM–3:30AM 🚌 96

D D'S CAFÉ
Spacious place where you can dance to a resident jazz band and eat a barbecue on the lawn in summer.
✚ E5 ✉ 639 Huashan Lu ☎ 6248 1118 🕐 6PM–3AM 🚌 48

DRAGON PUB
Partly decorated in Chinese style, this pub has a welcoming ambience and comfortable seating. Snacks are served.
✚ G5 ✉ 508 Julu Lu ☎ 6247 7453 🕐 10:30PM–midnight 🚌 42, 104

GALAXY
Two floors and a sizeable dance floor, with foreign

DJs playing the music of the moment.

➕ B6 ✉ Galaxy Hotel, 888 Zhongshan Xilu ☎ 6275 2999 Ext 2380 ⏰ 9PM–3AM 🚌 48, 72, 73

HYLAND 505 BREWERY

Recreated German Brauhaus—brick and stone interior and copper vats—serving good beer and snacks from a good location in a hotel on the Nanking Road.

➕ K5 ✉ Hotel Sofitel Hyland, 505 Nanjing Donglu ☎ 6351 5888 ⏰ 11PM–1AM 🚌 37

JURASSIC PUB

A little gloomy from the outside but a friendly, if eccentric, bar inside. The primeval theme extends to all aspects of the décor—everything is in the shape of dinosaurs, including the men's urinals. Snacks, including *teppanyaki* (Japanese grills), are served upstairs.

➕ G6 ✉ 8 Maoming Nanlu ☎ 6258 3758 ⏰ 2PM–4AM 🚌 126

KOWLOON CLUB'S LONGBAR DISCO

A joint venture taking up a lot of space in one of the buildings of the old Shanghai Exhibition Center.

➕ G5 ✉ 1333 Nanjing Xilu ☎ 6279 0279 Ext 7110 🚌 37

LAFAYETTE BAR

Sophisticated bar with a Scottish feel conveyed through the wood paneling and tartan decorations. Bar, snacks and MTV on the first floor, billiards on the second floor.

➕ E6 ✉ 76 Fuxing Xilu ☎ 6471 0937 ⏰ 2PM–2AM 🚌 96

L. A. PUB

Small bar that's relaxing and friendly for a drink away from the hurly-burly of the Huaihai Road.

➕ G6 ✉ 15 Shanxi Nanlu ☎ 6258 0546 ⏰ 2PM–3AM 🚌 42

NEW YORK NEW YORK

One of the most popular discos in town with a good mix of foreigners and locals.

➕ K4 ✉ 146 Huqiu Lu ☎ 6321 6097 ⏰ 8PM–5AM 🚌 21

O'MALLEY'S IRISH PUB

Irish beer is available in an old Shanghai house which has been renovated and transformed into an "antique" pub.

➕ E6 ✉ 42 Taojiang Lu ☎ 6437 0667 🚌 93

SHANGHAI SALLY'S

English-style pub offering pub food as well as a comprehensive range of drinks and various games.

➕ H6 ✉ 4 Xiangshan Lu ☎ 6327 1859 🚌 24

TOTAL DISCO PUB

Close to the People's Park, this is a lively disco popular with the locals.

➕ H5 ✉ 80 Xinchang Lu ☎ 6359 1635 ⏰ 9PM–4AM 🚌 109

TRIBESMAN PUB

Out of the way, but a good place to hear local bands (rock and jazz) perform.

➕ M2 ✉ 2150 Siping Lu ⏰ 7PM–4AM 🚌 100

Jazz

For a long time, the only faintly sensuous experience to be had in Shanghai was to listen and dance to the old jazz band in the Peace Hotel. Somehow, the tradition of playing trad jazz and swing music survived the long years of ideological rectitude, and in the new Shanghai a jazz band still plays nightly in the hotel's downstairs bar.

New club scene

Shanghai is on an upward swing and new clubs and bars are appearing all the time. To obtain the latest information, look in *Shanghai Talk*, the local events magazine, or *Culture & Recreation*, which is a sort of newsletter covering items of interest for visitors.

MOVIES, MUSIC & THEATER

Opera

Chinese opera is completely unlike Western opera. Foreigners find it difficult to appreciate it at first, but it is worth trying at least once. The singing style is falsetto and the action heavily stylized, but overall it is very colorful and can be highly dramatic, especially if battles are staged using acrobatic techniques. If you want to experience the opera while in Shanghai, check the local press for performances and venues.

MOVIES

CHINA THEATER
Movie theater offering a mixture of imported and home-grown movies.
✚ J4 ✉ 704 Niuzhuang Lu
☎ 6327 4260 🚌 25

GRAND CINEMA
One of the main movie theaters in the city showing Hollywood and Chinese movies.
✚ J5 ✉ 216 Nanjing Xilu
☎ 6327 3399 🚌 20, 27

MALONE'S BAR
Weekly movie shows (American and European) take place here, usually on a Wednesday.
✚ F4 ✉ 257 Tongren Lu
☎ 6247 2400

SHANGHAI FILM ART CENTER
Specializing in Chinese movies and dubbed foreign movies.
✚ D6 ✉ 160 Xinhua Lu
☎ 6280 6088 🚌 48

MUSIC

SHANGHAI CONSERVATORY OF MUSIC
Regular performances of classical Chinese and Western music take place most Sunday evenings at a conservatory now turning out international stars.
✚ F6 ✉ 20 Fenyang Lu
☎ 6437 0137 ext.2166 🚌 96

THEATER
China's acrobatic traditions go back at least 2,000 years. Although innovations include motorcycles and the unfortunate use of giant pandas, in essence the genius of the many acrobatic troupes throughout China lies in the skill of the performers and the simple nature of the props they use. Comedy is an important element—for example a performer balances upside down on the head of another, mimicking, as in a mirror, his partner's every movement.

LYCEUM THEATER
This pre-war theater where many of the world-famous stars of the era performed is now a temporary home to the Shanghai Acrobatic Troupe.
✚ G5–6 ✉ 57 Maoming Nanlu
☎ 6217 8530 🚌 42, 48

SHANGHAI CENTER THEATER
New theater giving regular performances of Chinese opera (➤ panel this page).
✚ F–G5 ✉ Shanghai Center, 1376 Nanjing Xilu ☎ 6279 8600 🚌 20, 27

SHANGHAI PEOPLE'S ART THEATER
This is an older theater showing movies and also putting on occasional musical performances.
✚ E6 ✉ 284 Anfu Lu
☎ 6322 5413 🚌 49

LUXURY HOTELS

GARDEN HOTEL
Close to the Huaihai Road, this hotel has grown up behind the façade of the old French Club. It has three restaurants, including a Japanese one, a business center and a health club.

✚ G6 ✉ 58 Maoming Nanlu
☎ 6415 1111; fax 6415 8866
🚍 41

JIN JIANG TOWER
The more recent version of the the old Jin Jiang down the street (▶ 82), the Jin Jiang Tower is a distinctive Shanghai landmark in the old French Concession, not far from the Huaihai Road. It contains several restaurants including Korean, Japanese and Italian, a business center and a recreation center.

✚ G6 ✉ 161 Changle Lu
☎ 6415 1188; fax 6415 0048
🚍 41

PORTMAN SHANGRI-LA
This hotel in the western section of the Nanjing Road forms part of the Shanghai Center, which is home to stores, restaurants and consulates. The hotel itself has a number of international restaurants, a florist, a gift store, a health club and a business center.

✚ G5 ✉ 1376 Nanjing Xilu
☎ 6279 8888; fax 6279 8800
🚍 20, 37

SHANGHAI HILTON
With all the hallmarks for which the chain is famous, the Hilton is fairly well located close to the Jing'an Temple and the western part of the Nanking Road. It has a number of restaurants, including two featuring Shanghai and Italian cooking, and a business center.

✚ F5 ✉ 250 Huashan Lu
☎ 6248 0000; fax 6248 3848
🚍 45

SHANGHAI JC MANDARIN
Offering luxury in the mold of the famous Hong Kong Mandarin, this hotel has a business center and fitness center, as well as a number of restaurants and bars.

✚ G5 ✉ 1225 Nanjing Xilu
☎ 6279 1888; fax 6279 1822
🚍 20, 37

SHERATON HUA TING
In the southwest of the city close to the Xujiahui Cathedral, the Sheraton is a large, well-established hotel with business and fitness centers, shopping arcade, beauty salon, disco and five restaurants.

✚ C9 ✉ 1200 Caoxi Beilu
☎ 6439 1000; fax 6255 0830
🏊 Gymnasium 🚍 42, 43, 73

WESTIN TAI PING YANG
This comfortable hotel is conveniently placed for the airport, on the western edge of the city. There are six restaurants (including Italian and Japanese), a health club and a business center.

✚ B5 ✉ 5 Zunyi Lu
☎ 6275 8888; fax 6275 5420
🚍 57

Hotel prices
Approximate prices for a double room:

Budget	250–750 yuan
Mid-range	750–1,500 yuan
Luxury over	1,500 yuan

Bills
Whenever you check out from your hotel, look through the bill very carefully. If a previous tenant of your room has succeeded in leaving without having paid for telephone calls, for example, these may find their way onto your bill.

MID-RANGE & BUDGET HOTELS

Bargains

In general, hotels in Shanghai are pretty expensive. But competition is fierce, so don't be afraid to ask for discounts or special deals—no hotel will voluntarily offer a lower price or advertise that it is half empty, but may offer a discount which, no matter how small, is always welcome.

MID-RANGE HOTELS

EQUATORIAL HOTEL

High-rise hotel, not far from the western part of the Nanking Road, with a Bavarian Steak House, Italian, Japanese and Cantonese restaurants, and a 24-hour café (➤ 69). Also a gym, swimming pool, sauna, and tennis and squash courts.

➕ F5 ✉ 65 Yan'an Xilu ☎ 6248 1688; fax 6248 1773 🚌 71

HOLIDAY INN CROWNE PLAZA

Reasonably good location in the western part of the city and with all the good-value facilities associated with this chain. Several restaurants, a well-regarded bar (➤ 78), a delicatessen, indoor swimming pool, sauna and tennis club.

➕ D6 ✉ 400 Fanyu Lu ☎ 6280 8888; fax 6280 2788 🚌 76

HOTEL SOFITEL HYLAND

In a busy part of the Nanking Road, within easy walking distance of the Bund. Business center, fitness center, sauna, delicatessen, German bar and several restaurants, including one specializing in Shanghai cooking.

➕ K5 ✉ 505 Nanjing Donglu ☎ 6351 5888; fax 6351 4088 🚌 37

JING AN HOTEL

Goodish location close to where the western portion of the Nanking Road meets the Yan'an Road.

The modernized former "Haig Apartments" has restaurants specializing in seafood and Shanghai cooking, a health center, post office, beauty salon and business center.

➕ F5 ✉ 370 Huashan Lu ☎ 6248 1888; fax 6248 2657 🚌 45, 48

JIN JIANG

Historic pre-war hotel in the old style in the former French Concession, close to the Huaihai Road. All twin-bedded rooms. Several restaurants, a 24-hour coffee store and a number of good stores.

➕ G6 ✉ 59 Maoming Nanlu ☎ 6258 2582; fax 6472 5588 🚌 26

OCEAN HOTEL

Good location overlooking the Huangpu, not too far from the Bund. A revolving restaurant at the top serves Sichuan cooking; disco, shopping arcade and recreation center.

➕ N4 ✉ 1171 Dongdaming Lu ☎ 6545 8888; fax 6545 8993 🚌 28

PEACE HOTEL

The classic Shanghai hotel (➤ 46) with a wonderful location on the Bund. Modernization has not been completely sympathetic, but the hotel's position and historical associations are hard to beat. Business center, gym, sauna, billiards, several restaurants and, of course, the famous jazz bar.

➕ K5 ✉ 20 Nanjing Donglu ☎ 6321 6888; fax 6329 0300 🚌 27

RADISSON SAS LANSHENG

Not a great location in the northern part of the city, but very good value and very comfortable with large rooms. Business center, lobby bar, disco and several restaurants, including an excellent Chinese buffet.

✚ Off map to northeast
✉ 1000 Quyang Lu ☎ 6542 8000; fax 6544 8400

BUDGET HOTELS

China is notorious for the lack of budget hotels. The reason for this is that the Chinese tend to concentrate on the upper end of the market (even during the early 1980s, when there were no good hotels at all, prices were high). Shanghai is particularly bad in this respect and the only really cheap accommodation is in those few places with dormitories. Many of the following hotels cannot be truly classed as budget— they are merely among the cheaper ones. Otherwise, ask for discounts and keep your fingers crossed(▶ panel).

DONG FENG HOTEL

In an excellent location on the Bund, the former Shanghai Club is very cheap by Chinese standards if little seedy. Business center and several restaurants.

✚ K5 ✉ 3 Zhongshan Dongyilu ☎ 6321 8060; fax 6321 0261 🚌 42, 55

DONGHU

This reasonably priced hotel in the heart of the old French Concession occupies a pre-war building with links with the gangster Du Yuesheng. Several restaurants (Sichuan and Cantonese), swimming pool and tennis courts.

✚ F6 ✉ 70 Donghu Lu ☎ 6415 8158; fax 6415 7759 🚌 45

EAST ASIA HOTEL

Old-style building in an excellent location, providing inexpensive, simple rooms. A host of restaurants are available— Shanghai, Cantonese and French—plus a business center and shopping arcade.

✚ J5 ✉ 680 Nanjing Donglu ☎ 6322 3223; fax 6322 4598 🚌 37

HENGSHAN

Old modernized hotel in the southwest of the city. Several restaurants (including one serving French cuisine, and others offering Sichuan and Shanghai styles), business center, sauna, gym and supermarket.

✚ D7 ✉ 534 Hengshan Lu ☎ 6437 7050; fax 6433 5732 🚌 42

HEXIN HOTEL

Simple hotel with 245 rooms which is located close to the railroad station. Facilities include a business center, clinic, beauty salon, ticket reservation service and Chinese restaurants.

✚ J3 ✉ Gonghexin Lu ☎ 5665 2250; fax 5665 2378 🚌 46, 95, 108, 114

Reservations

If you are on a tight budget, it is best not to arrive in Shanghai without a hotel reservation. Budget accommodation is in fairly short supply, and wandering about this huge city with luggage could prove time consuming and expensive.

83

JIN JIANG YMCA HOTEL

Good central location and reasonably priced rooms. Gym, business center and a couple of restaurants.

✚ J6 ✉ 123 Xizang Nanlu ☎ 6326 1040; fax 6320 1957 🚌 17, 18, 23

METROPOLE

Well placed very close to the Nanking Road and the Bund, this hotel in a pre-war building is comfortable and good value. Beauty salon, business center, sauna and gym.

✚ K5 ✉ 180 Jiangxi Zhonglu ☎ 6321 3030; fax 6321 7365 🚌 64

PARK HOTEL

Classic old pre-war skyscraper, modernized a little garishly. Excellent location and facilities which include a business center, shopping arcade, beauty salon and several restaurants.

✚ J5 ✉ 170 Nanjing Xilu ☎ 6327 5225; fax 6327 6958 🚌 20, 37

PUJIANG HOTEL

One of the best options for the budget-conscious traveler, the Pujiang was once the Astor Hotel and is just beyond the north end of the Bund. Dormitory accommodation is available, as well as cheap twin rooms.

✚ L4 ✉ 15 Huangpu Lu ☎ 6324 6388; fax 6324 3179 🚌 28

SEVENTH HEAVEN

Distinctive pre-war building on the Nanking Road at very reasonable prices. Rooms are fairly well equipped while facilities include a business center, clinic, post office and a number of restaurants including Cantonese and Sichuan.

✚ J5 ✉ Nanjing Dong Lu ☎ 6322 0777; fax 6351 7193 🚌 27

SHANGCHUAN HOTEL

New, reasonably priced hotel in the newly developed area of Pudong, opposite the Bund. It has 74 rooms, a business center, billiard room, shopping center and a restaurant specializing in Sichuan and Yangzhou cooking.

✚ N6 ✉ 3 Jimo Lu, Pudong ☎ 5884 0451; fax 5884 0869 🚌 81, 85

SHANGHAI MANSIONS

Formerly Broadway Mansions, this ziggurat-like hotel stands just beyond the northern end of the Bund. A number of restaurants, including a Japanese one, a business center, a beauty salon, billiard room and shopping arcade.

✚ L4 ✉ 20 Bei Suzhou Lu ☎ 6324 6260; fax 6306 5147 🚌 65

SHANGHAI PACIFIC HOTEL

Excellently positioned on Nanking Road, this hotel has a piano bar, two restaurants (Western and Fujian) and a business center.

✚ J5 ✉ 104 Nanjing Xilu ☎ 6327 6226; fax 6399 3634 🚌 20, 27

SHANGHAI
travel facts

Arriving & Departing

When to go

- The best time to visit Shanghai is either in the spring (late April/May) or in the late summer or early fall. At both times, the days are often clear and warm and therefore comfortable for exploring the city on foot which is the best way of coming across the sort of detail that tells Shanghai's singular story.
- Spring is the season when the parks are filled with fruit blossom.
- Fall is the season for Shanghai crab, a speciality of the city.
- Most visitors arrive in the hot summer months, but at least nowadays most hotels and stores are air-conditioned.

Before you go

- Visitors must hold a valid passport with at least six months' validity.
- Visas for all foreign nationals must be obtained in advance from the nearest Chinese Consulate or Embassy. They are valid for 30 days but can be extended once you arrive in China. Allow five days for its issue. A passport photograph and fee will be required. If in a group you may be traveling on a group visa.
- In Shanghai visa extensions are issued by the Public Security Bureau, 233 Hankou Lu.
- No vaccinations are required unless traveling from a yellow fever infected area. However, doctors may recommend inoculation against hepatitis A

Climate

- Shanghai enjoys a northern subtropical maritime climate and has four seasons.
- Winter (November to February) is fairly cold and dry although it is rare for temperatures to fall below freezing.
- Late spring is pleasant. Trees begin to blossom in April. May is usually comfortably warm but often wet.
- Summer is extremely hot and humid with average temperatures approaching 82°F in July and August.
- September and October are often pleasantly warm, although September is also one of the wetter months.

Arriving by air

- Hongqiao International Airport is 11 miles west of the city center.
- The best way of getting to the center is by taxi which will cost approximately 70 yuan.
- CAAC (Civil Airline Administration of China) runs a shuttle bus between the airport and its office on Yan'an Lu.
- A new airport is under construction in Pudong.

Arriving by boat

- The journey from Hong Kong takes approximately three days.
- The boats on the Hong Kong–Shanghai route are well appointed although you are advised to obtain the best cabin you can afford and to insure that you have enough cash to pay for bar bills and other extras. There are lounge areas, sun decks and, usually, a swimming pool. The food is Chinese.
- The journey along China's east coast may be your best opportunity to see traditional fishing junks.

Traveling by boat

- There are regular departures to other coastal cities, e.g. Ningbo and the holy island of Putuoshan.

- Tickets for boat journeys can be purchased via CITS in Hong Kong and Shanghai.

Arriving by train

- Shanghai's main station is in the north of the city on Jiaotong Lu.
- Taxis are readily available at the station.
- Remember to retain your ticket until you are out of the terminal.
- Train travel is recommended as a way of seeing the surrounding countryside, or venturing around China. There are, broadly speaking, two classes, so-called hard- and soft-classes.
- Soft-class has more privacy (on sleepers), more comfort and may occasionally be air-conditioned.
- Many long-distance trains have restaurant cars where the standard of cooking is perhaps better than might be expected. On other trains, there may be vendors selling tea, snacks and souvenirs.
- One route that is recommended for its scenic beauty is between Shanghai and Canton, passing through gorgeous subtropical scenery during the southern part of the journey.

Customs regulations

- You may import 600 cigarettes, 2 liters of alcohol, 0.5 liters of perfume.
- When departing, be careful that any antique you have purchased is permitted to leave the country. Antiques that are permitted for export must bear a red seal and any item not carrying the seal may be seized at customs.

Departure/airport tax

- 50 RMB for domestic flights, 90 RMB for international flights.

ESSENTIAL FACTS

Electricity

- 220V, 50 cycles AC.
- Plugs come in a variety of types, the most common being the two flat pinned type. It is worth taking an adaptor with you.

Etiquette

- It might be thought that in China, as Japan, there are elaborate codes of conduct. However, most traditional etiquette was swept away in the wake of the revolution and nowadays etiquette is less important than general approach.
- Avoid displays of anger and aggression. These do not go down well in China, where intemperance is considered to be a sign of weakness.
- If you have a complaint, gentle, persistent questioning is the best way of dealing with it.
- Certain subjects (e.g. sex and politics) are, if not taboo, close to being so. Remember that, despite appearances, China is a totalitarian country and unorthodox opinions are discouraged.
- The language barrier means that irony is wasted and you may be placed in the embarrassing position of having to explain what was intended merely as a wry observation.
- Though the niceties of table etiquette continue to be observed at banquets (during which the emphasis is on presentation and service), by many standards table manners are non-existent. Spitting and hawking, furthermore, are still widespread and cigarette smoking very common.

Tipping

- Despite official disapproval, tipping is no longer an offence.

Indeed it is now expected by tourist guides who prefer money—American dollars are favorites—to any well-intentioned gift. Hotel porters wil usually happily accept a tip, and so will taxi drivers although it is not necessarily expected. In most restaurants, tips are not usually expected, except in some of the top establishments.

Insurance
- Travel insurance covering medical expenses is essential.
- In the event of medical treatment, be sure to keep all receipts.

Money Matters
- The currency is the Reminbi (RMB), of which the basic unit is the "yuan" (or, colloquially, the "kwai") divided into 100 fen. Ten fen is sometimes considered as a single unit known as a "jiao" or "mao."
- There are coins of 1 yuan, 5 jiao, 1 jiao, 5 fen, 2 fen, 1 fen. Notes come in denominations of 100, 50, 10, 5 and 2 yuan.
- Money can be changed in most hotels. A passport may be required.
- Credit cards are accepted in international hotels and stores but not in the Chinese equivalent of the "corner store."
- RMB can be changed back into foreign currency when leaving China, but you must produce relevant exchange receipts.

National Holidays
- Some holidays are calculated according to the variable nature of the Lunar calendar.
- New Year's Day (January 1).
- Chinese New Year or Spring Festival. Usually in February.
- International Working Women's

Day (March 8).
- International Labor Day (May 1).
- Youth Day (May 4).
- Children's Day (June 1).
- Anniversary of the founding of the Army of People's Republic of China (July 1).
- Anniversary of the founding of the People's Republic of China (August 1).
- National Day (October 1).

Opening hours
- Offices: variable, but in general Mon–Sat 9–12, 2–5.
- Banks: Mon–Sat 9–12, 2–5.
- Stores: variable, but in general most stores are open every day 9–6.

Places of worship
- Buddhist: Jade Buddha Temple
  - ✉ 170 Anyuan Lu
  - ☎ 6266 3668.
- Longhua Temple
  - ✉ 2853 Longhua Lu
  - ☎ 6457 1440.
- Catholic: Xujiahui Cathedral
  - ✉ 158 Puxi Lu
  - ☎ 5637 1328.
- Interdenominational: Muen Interdenominational Church
  - ✉ 316 Xizang Zhonglu
  - ☎ 622 5069.
- Muslim: Xiao Taoyuan Mosque
  - ✉ 52 Xiaotaoyuan Jie
  - ☎ 677 5442.

Photography
- Photography is forbidden in most museums, but some institutions permit it on payment of a fee in advance. There is stiff fine for those who do not comply.
- Color print film is widely available, black-and-white or slide film much less so.
- Video film can be found but not always easily.
- All security X-ray machines in

China are film-safe.
- The atmosphere in Shanghai is often hazy and filters are advisable.

Student travelers

- An International Student Card is not a great deal of help in China. However, the occasional concession may be available, so carry one with you, backed up by your home Student Card and a letter from college.

Time difference

- Shanghai is 13 hours ahead of New York, 8 hours ahead of GMT, 13 hours ahead of New York and 2 hours behind Melbourne.

Toilets

- You will find Western-style toilets are common in hotels and in many restaurants, but the traditional hole in the ground is also common.
- Public toilets are not generally available and those that do exist can be distinctly unsanitary. More and better facilities are gradually appearing, but you are advised to carry your own paper and soap.

Tourist Offices

- China does not have tourist information offices. Most people still travel in groups, so the main source of information will be from local guides. Individual travelers have to rely on their own ingenuity. The China International Travel Service (CITS, the state-run travel service) is becoming more professional in its outlook and will often help even when you are not organizing your trip through them. Otherwise, try an independent agent.

Overseas Tourist Offices

- Australia:
  ✉ 55 Clarence St., Sydney NSW 2000
  ☎ (02) 9299 4057; fax (02) 9290 1958

- Canada:
  ✉ 480 University Avenue, Suite 806, Toronto, Ontario, M5G 1V2
  ☎ (416) 599 6636; fax (416) 599 6382
- Hong Kong:
  ✉ Tower Two, South Seas Center, 75 Mody Road, Tsimshatsui East, Kowloon
  ☎ 732 5888; fax721 7154
- UK:
  ✉ 4 Glentworth Street, London NW1 5PG
  ☎ (0171) 935 9427; fax (0171) 487 5842
- USA, Los Angeles:
  ✉ 333 West Broadway, Suite 201, Glendale, CA 91204
  ☎ (818) 545 7505; fax (818) 545 7506.
- USA, New York:
  ✉ Lincoln Building, 60E, 42nd Street, Suite 3126, New York, NY 10165
  ☎ (212) 867 0271; fax: (212) 599 2892

Local tourist information:

- China International Travel Service: ✉ 8th floor No. 1277 Beijing lu
  ☎ 6321 7200
- Tourist hotline ☎ 6252 0000

Women travelers

- In general, China is a very safe place for foreign women. Incidents of harassment or worse are few and far between, but it is perhaps as well to note that most Chinese women are still fairly modest in their dress.

Lone travelers

- China is still difficult for lone travelers on a budget. CITS are not especially helpful and there is very little accommodation that can be classed as truly inexpensive.

Visitors with disabilities

- China is not a country that has made many concessions to people with disabilities. However, very slowly, things are improving. As new hotels and museums are constructed, so access is being made easier for wheelchair users and

89

wheelchairs are more readily available at airports. However, attitudes, in general, are not thoughtful or considerate—you should be prepared for difficulties and for the need to improvise.

PUBLIC TRANSPORTATION

General information

- Whenever possible, the best way of getting around Shanghai, in order to get to know it in detail, is on foot. Obviously, in such a large city this is not always feasible, in which case you are recommended to use taxis.

Buses

- The comprehensive bus service is very cheap, but the buses can be extremely crowded, especially close to the rush hour.
- Buses run between 5AM and 11PM.
- The best tourist bus routes are: the No. 11 which shuttles around the Old Town; the No. 16 which runs between the banks of the Huangpu and the Old Town and the Jade Buddha Temple; the No. 18 which runs between the railroad station, Xizang Lu, and the river; and the No. 65 which runs betweeen the Bund and close to the railroad station.
- Make sure that you have small change—you pay your fare on board.
- Note that pushing one's way on board is a feature of daily life. Pickpockets are not unknown.

Subway

- Payment is made in advance at kiosks.
- Trains run up to every 9 minutes.
- One section (from Station via Renmin Square and Huaihai Lu to the south of the city) was completed in 1995. A new section, running along the Nanking Road and linking the airport with Pudong is under construction.

Taxis

- Taxis are widely available, metered and easy to flag down.
- Travel by taxi is very inexpensive and definitely the best way of getting around, occasional traffic jams notwithstanding.
- In general, Shanghai taxi drivers are very honest. However, if you are dissatisfied, take note of the license number displayed inside.

Bicycles

- Bicycles (*zixingche*) are widely used and can be rented at little cost in most cities in or at specialist outlets.
- Check the brakes and tires before setting out and observe how the traffic functions in China—joining it unprepared can be an unnerving experience.
- Wayside repairs can often easily be effected by mechanics who ply their trade on the pavement.

Where to get maps

- Basic tourist maps of Shanghai are widely available from bookstores, hotels and CITS.

MEDIA & COMMUNICATIONS

Media

- International newspapers (usually the *International Herald Tribune*) and magazines are widely available from hotel newsstands.
- Satellite television (e.g. BBC, Star, CNN) is available in many hotels.
- Voice of America and BBC World Service can be picked up on short-wave radios.
- China's English language paper is

the *China Daily*, available free in most hotels. *Shanghai Talk* and *Culture & Recreation* are English language publications with news and listings for foreign visitors to Shanghai.
- There is a Shanghai web-site at http://www.shanghai-ed.com/j_whats.htm.

Post offices
- The main post office is on the corner of Suzhou Beilu and Sichuan Lu.
- The Poste Restante address is 276 Suzhou Beilu.
- Stamps can be purchased from most hotels.
- Mail boxes are normally green; but your best bet is to mail from the hotel by handing in letters at reception.
- The postal service is very efficient and most mail should take no longer than 10 days to reach anywhere in the world.

Telephones
- Local calls can be made from public phone booths all over the city for a small charge.
- Long-distance domestic calls can be made from phone booths but not usually international calls.
- Local calls from hotel rooms are often free. International direct dialing is normally available but is expensive.
- Card phones are gradually being introduced.
- The international access code from China is 00. Alternatively, call 108 to get through to a local operator in the country being called, through whom a collect call can be made.
- Most tourist class hotels upwards have facilities for sending faxes, and more and more are acquiring them for sending e-mail.

EMERGENCIES

Consulates
- Australia:
  ✉ 17 Fuxing Xilu ☎ 6433 4604
- Canada:
  ✉ Suite 604, West Tower, Shanghai Center, 1376 Nanjing Xilu ☎ 6279 8400
- New Zealand:
  ✉ 15B, Qihua Tower, 1375 Huaihai Zhonglu ☎ 6433 2230
- UK:
  ✉ 244 Yongfu Lu ☎ 6433 0508
- USA:
  ✉ 1469 Huaihai Lu ☎ 6433 6880

Emergency phone numbers
- Ambulance ☎ 120
- Fire ☎ 119
- Police ☎ 110

Lost property
- If you lose an item of value, you should contact the Public Security Bureau ✉ 210 Hankou Lu ☎ 6321 5380, or the organization through whom your visa was obtained (e.g. if you are a tourist, go to CITS).

Medical treatment
- Treatment is available in state hospitals and in private, joint-venture clinics.
- For minor ailments, the foreigner section of the state-run hospitals will normally be the cheapest option. However, this is variable and you are advised to try to ascertain the cost of treatment in advance.
- Your host organization (e.g. CITS) or hotel will help to put you in contact with a hospital.
- Private clinics:
  New Pioneer Medical Center
  ✉ 910 Hengshan Lu
  ☎ 6469 3898;
  World Link Medical Center
  ✉ Shanghai Centre, 1376 Nanjing Xilu;

Sino-Canadian Dental Centre
✉ Ninth People's Hospital, 639 Zhizao Julu
☎ 6313 31741 ext. 5276;
Shanghai Ko Sei Dental Clinic,
✉ 666 Changle Lu
☎ 6247 7000.

- State hospitals:
Hua Dong Hospital,
Foreigners' Clinic,
✉ 257 Yan'an Xilu
☎ 6248 3180 ext. 3106;
Huashan Hospital, Foreigners'
Clinic,
✉ 12 Wulumuqi Zhonglu
☎ 6248 3986;
IMCC in First People's Hospital
✉ 85 Wujun lu
☎ 6324 0090 ext. 2101;
Pediatric Hospital, Foreigners'
Clinic
✉ Shanghai Medical University, 183 Fenglin Lu
☎ 6403 7371.

Medicines

- Western medicines are available
but can be expensive. Traditional
Chinese medicine is effective but
often slow to take effect.
- If you have particular medical
needs, make sure that you are
equipped to satisfy them before
you visit China.

Sensible precautions

- Shanghai is generally safe.
Pickpockets do exist, however,
so be cautious. Conceal
valuables when on the street.
- Make use of hotel safes and take
out only what you need.
- Beware of black marketeers on
the streets.
- Antiques older than about 150
years cannot be exported from
China. Genuine, exportable
antiques will have a seal on
them.

LANGUAGE

English is widely spoken in hotels
and in places where foreigners con-
gregate. In general, however, you will
find that little English is spoken. The
official language of China is known as
Mandarin in the West, or "*putonghua*"
in China, and is based on the dialect
of Beijing. It is spoken throughout
China, but local dialects are com-
monly used—the Shanghai dialect is
very different from *putonghua*.
However, knowledge of a few
putonghua words and phrases will
undoubtedly be an advantage at some
point.

Pronunciation

- The modern phonetic romanized
form of Chinese is called "pinyin."
It is largely pronounced as written,
but note the following:
a as in c*a*r
c as in bi*ts* when an initial conso-
nant
e as in h*e*r
i as in f*ee*t unless preceded by c, ch,
r, s, sh, z, sh, when it becomes *er* as
in her
j as in *g*in
o as in f*o*rd
q like the ch in *ch*in
s as in *s*imple
u as in oo in c*oo*l
w as in *w*ade, though pronounced
by some as v
x like the sh in *sh*eep but with the s
given greater emphasis
y as in *y*oyo
z as in ds in li*ds*; zh as j in jam

Greetings

hello/how are you	ni hao
please	qing
thank you	xiexie
goodbye	zai jian
cheers!	gan bei
no problem	mei wen tí
I'm fine	wo hen hao

My surname is…	Wo xing…
I am from	Who shi…laide
Are you married?	Ni jiehunle ma?

Hotel

hotel	binguan, fandian
room	fang jian
bathroom	xishu jian

Post office, bank, stores

post office	youju
stamp	you piao
postcard	ming xin pian
airmail	hang kong
letter	xin
telephone	dianhua
bank	yin hang
money exchange	huan qian chu
how much?	Duo shao qian?
too expensive	tai gui le
a little cheaper	pian yi dian ba
gift	li wu
credit card	xin yong ka
antique	guwu
silk	sichou
jade	yu
carpet	di tan
rice	mifan
beer	pijiu
coffee	ka fei

Restaurant

restaurant fan guan, fan dian, can ting

do you have a menu in English? you mei you ying wen cai dan?

water/cooled boiled water shui/liang kai shui

coffee	kafei
black tea	hong cha
beer	pi jiu
soft drink	qi shui
rice	mi fan
fork	cha zi

Getting around

bus	gong gong qi che
bus station	qi che zhan
boat	chuan
bicycle	zixing che

taxi	chu zu qi che
train	huo che
toilet	cesuo

Emergency

I feel sick	wo bu shu fu
I would like	wo xiang
doctor	yi sheng
aspirin	zhitongpian
hospital	yiyuan
pharmacy	yaodian

General

good/OK	hao
not good/bad	Bu hao
to buy	mai
ticket	piao
receipt	fa piao
no/not have/ there is not/there are
not	mei you
I	wo
he/she	ta
we	women
you	ni/nimen
they	tamen
how much?	duo sha qian?
where is?	zai nar?
is there anyone who speaks English?
you mei you ren hui shuo yin wen?
today	jin tian
yesterday	zuo tian
tomorrow	ming tian
evening	wan shang
afternoon	xia wu
left	zuo
right	you
please write it down	qing xie

Numbers

0	ling	9	jiu
1	yi, yao	10	shi
2	er, liang	11	shiyi
3	san	12	shier
4	si	20	ershi
5	wu	21	ershiyi
6	liu	100	yibai
7	qi	200	erbai
8	ba	1,000	yiqian

INDEX

CityPack
Shanghai

While every care has been taken to ensure the accuracy of the information in this guide, time brings change, and consequently the publisher cannot accept responsibility for errors that may occur. Prudent travelers will therefore want to call ahead to verify prices and other "perishable" information.

Copyright   © 1999 by The Automobile Association
Maps copyright   © 1999 by The Automobile Association
Fold-out map: © RV Reise- und Verkehrsverlag Munich · Stuttgart
                  © Cartography: GeoData

Published in the United States by Fodor's Travel Publications, Inc.
Published in the United Kingdom by AA Publishing

Fodor's is a registered trademark of Fodor's Travel Publications, Inc.

ISBN 0–679–00262–6
First Edition

FODOR'S CITYPACK SHANGHAI

AUTHOR *Christopher Knowles*
COVER DESIGN *Fabrizio La Rocca,*
              Allison Saltzman
VERIFIER *Lu Jun*
AMERICANIZER *Chester Krone*

CARTOGRAPHY *The Automobile Association*
             RV Reise- und Verkehrsverlag
COPY EDITOR *Audrey Horne*
INDEXER *Marie Lorimer*

Acknowledgments

Christopher Knowles would like to thank Leszek Szteinduchert of Voyages Jules Verne for his help in making travel arrangements, and Tong Wei of CITS.
The Automobile Association wishes to thank the following photographers and libraries for their assistance in the preparation of this book:

Hulton Getty, 12; Neil Setchfield, 5a, 5b, 7, 46b, 63b

The remaining photos are held in the Association's own photo library (AA Photo Library) and were taken by Gordon Clements with the exception of pages 13b, 18, 20, 22, 23, 25a, 44a, 50a, 51a, 60 and 85b which were taken by Alex Kouprianoff and pages 9, 21, 41a taken by Ingrid Morejohn.

Special sales

Color separation by Daylight Colour Art Pte Ltd, Singapore
Manufactured by Dai Nippon Printing Co. (Hong Kong) Ltd
10 9 8 7 6 5 4 3 2 1

Titles in the Citypack series

- Amsterdam • Atlanta • Beijing • Berlin • Boston • Chicago • Dublin •
- Florence • Hong Kong • London • Los Angeles • Madrid • Miami •
- Montréal • Moscow • New York • Paris • Prague • Rome • San Francisco •
- Seattle • Shanghai • Sydney • Tokyo • Toronto • Venice • Vienna •
- Washington DC •